Strong,
Smart,
& Bold

This book
is a gift from
The Teacher Center
In memory of
Corinne Levin

Strong,  Smart,

Empowering Girls for Life

& Bold

Carla Fine
Foreword by Jane Fonda

 girls inc.

Cliff Street Books
An Imprint of HarperCollins*Publishers*

HarperCollins books may be purchased for educational, business, or sales promotional use. For information please write: Special Markets Department, HarperCollins Publishers Inc., 10 East 53rd Street, New York, NY 10022.

FIRST EDITION

Designed by Claire Vaccaro

Library of Congress Cataloging-in-Publication Data

Fine, Carla.
   Strong, smart and bold : empowering girls for life / by Carla Fine ;   foreword by Jane Fonda.—1st ed.
      p. cm.
   Includes bibliographical references.
   ISBN 0-06-019771-4
   1. Girls. 2. Parenting. 3 Girls—Conduct of life. 4. Women—Education. I. Title

HQ777 .F562000
649'.133—dc21

                                                                        00-064431
            01 02 03 04 05   RRD   10 9 8 7 6 5 4 3 2 1

*To my mother, Lillian Fine,
for her example of embracing life
to the fullest and celebrating each
new adventure with warmth and love.*

Contents

Acknowledgments   ix

Foreword
by Jane Fonda   xi

Introduction
Raising a Girl Who Knows Her Rights   1

Chapter One
Resisting Gender Stereotypes   9

Chapter Two
Speaking Freely and Openly   37

Chapter Three
Taking Risks and Achieving Goals   61

Chapter Four
Accepting and Appreciating One's Body   87

Chapter Five
Being Confident and Safe   113

Chapter Six
Preparing for Economic Independence   149

Conclusion
Creating an Equitable Society   171

Appendix A
101 Ways to Empower a Girl and
   Improve Her World   179

Appendix B
Resource Directory for Girls   195

Appendix C
References   201

Acknowledgments

I would like to thank everyone at Girls Inc., a remarkable organization whose unequivocal dedication to girls is backed up by hands-on programs and cutting-edge research. The commitment of the staff, board members, and affiliates of Girls Inc. is truly inspiring, and I consider it an honor to have worked with them on this book.

I am especially grateful to Isabel Carter Stewart, former president of Girls Inc., for encouraging this book from its inception and eloquently sharing her expertise and insights. In addition, the vast knowledge and practical experience of Maureen Bilger, Susan Houchin, Bernice Humphrey, Pat Loomes, Andrea Nemetz, Heather Johnston Nicholson, Jan Roberta, Jan Stanton, Brenda Stegall, Janet Street, Sandra Timmons, Lynne Tsuda, and Mildred Kiefer Wurf helped to inform every aspect of the book, and I appreciate their valuable input. A particular expression of gratitude to Alexander Kopelman and his Communications

Department staff for shepherding the book from the beginning and assisting with the many assorted details that go along with determining the ultimate success of such an undertaking.

It was truly a privilege to work with Jane Fonda—an inspiration to women and girls throughout the world. In her role as chair of the Girls Inc. Girls' Rights Campaign, Jane is not only changing the way society views and treats girls but also transforming how they regard themselves. Her voice sounds the note and we join with her proudly. I would also like to acknowledge Barbara Taylor Bradford and Herb Scannell, the other cochairs of the campaign, for their unwavering dedication and commitment.

I appreciate Ila Hess, Maya Hess, Kathleen Mahmood, Rose Wolner, Samantha Wolner, and all the girls I met from Girls Inc. affiliates across the country, for sharing their experiences with me. Thank you, again, to Aukia Betancourt, the girl in my life who is now a wonderful young woman.

As always, I am grateful for the help, insight, and encouragement of my agent and friend, Barbara Lowenstein. I also greatly appreciate the wise advice and astute guidance of my editors, Diane Reverand and Janet Dery.

A special thanks to Anastasia Higginbotham for her assistance with the book. Her knowledge, instincts, and professional skills are as admirable as her commitment to girls and their right to be strong, safe, and free.

My husband, Allen Oster, not only bounced around ideas and concepts for the book with me but also lent his fine editorial skills to the process. Allen's joy of life sustains me, and his unshakable support inspires me. I am blessed by his presence.

Foreword

by Jane Fonda

CHAIR, GIRLS INC. GIRLS' RIGHTS CAMPAIGN

When I was a little girl, I had lofty ambitions. I wanted to lead armies, to vanquish the bad guys, and be not the fairest but the bravest in the land. But something happened on my way to teenagehood. My spirit shrank to the size of a thimble. I became preoccupied with how I looked, with fitting in and being popular, especially with boys. I kept my deepest thoughts and feelings to myself because they no longer seemed suitable. After a while I didn't really know what I thought or felt. My inner voice grew silent.

As chair of the Girls Inc. Girls' Rights Campaign, I am passionately committed to making sure that girls' voices remain loud and that girls are valued for who they are, not who they pretend to be. The Girls' Bill of Rights is dedicated to advancing the basic human rights of girls: the right to be respected, self-reliant, healthy, and safe.

Girls are the agents of change. They are our most potent

force for making a difference in the world. They can reshape our society, change the rules, and transform our preconceived notions. They can do this if we are brave enough to allow them to maintain their voices and allow them to lead us on a journey of discovery and rediscovery.

An empowered girl not only knows and believes in her rights, she also advocates those rights for herself as well as others. Yet, even though the national Girls' Rights Survey conducted by Girls Inc. confirms that girls today are strong, smart, and bold, the poll also shows that girls still run into roadblocks that keep them from being their best selves.

There is tremendous pressure on girls to silence and sacrifice the courageous parts of themselves in order to stay in relationships they feel are important to them. The preeminent scholar Carol Gilligan, whose book *In a Different Voice* has changed the way we look at women and girls in our society, says that girls gradually lose their "ordinary courage" to speak out. Having a voice at all becomes extraordinary, and is usually experienced in only the safest and most private relationships.

Girls Inc. believes that it is the right of every girl to be able to speak her mind in a secure and accepting environment. Our job is to allow her voice to connect with our hearts, letting her know that we feel hers is a voice worth listening to and that we will not automatically judge her or criticize her if she tells us something that is hard for us to hear.

We must not only be mothers, we must also be "other-mothers," making sure that our nieces, our little sisters, our students, our mentees, our friends' daughters, as well our own daughters know that their voices are imprinted in our hearts and in our minds. We must show all girls that we treasure them as real people with valid opinions and real points of view.

The Girls' Bill of Rights is a new wave in the women's movement. We're now at a point in history where significant gains have been made and profound changes have been achieved. But there is also a danger of complacency, or even a gradual rollback of existing advances.

Educating girls about their rights and helping them to learn how to advocate for themselves is a way to protect our past gains and to move beyond them, breaking down the remaining barriers that stand in the way of full and equal participation in society.

A girl who is separated from her true voice grows into a woman who is no longer connected with herself, who leaves her power at the door, perhaps not in her professional or political life, but in her most intimate relationships. She unwittingly models this loss of self to her children, and so the cycle is repeated. I know this in my gut. It has taken me until my sixties to reclaim my voice and take what Carol Gilligan calls "the road back from selflessness."

I don't want today's girls to have to wait as long as I have waited. It is never too late to begin, but neither is it too early. Every girl in our increasingly connected world must be equipped with the tools and skills necessary to exercise and advocate for her rights. Every girl deserves our support and encouragement to maintain and sustain her voice. Let her voice help us to reclaim our own so that we can join with her in making the journey to full personhood.

Strong, Smart, & Bold

Introduction

Raising a Girl Who Knows Her Rights

Imagine a world where a girl is not limited by the fact that she was born female. She goes to school confident that her clothes, hair, and weight will not be discussed in the hallways. In class, she raises her hand high, not too intimidated about voicing her opinion. After school, she goes to basketball practice at the local recreation center, where the girls' team is cheered on as loudly as the boys' team. She walks home from practice confidently, without worrying that she might be a target for teasing or harassment. At night, she finishes her homework knowing that she can pursue careers that were closed to women in earlier generations.

The reality of a girl's life today is much different. The opportunities—and pressures—she faces are enormous: she plans to be a rocket scientist when she grows up but worries about her weight; she pitches for her school's softball team but is afraid of getting attacked in the locker room; she speaks at a national youth convention but is unable to tell her boyfriend she doesn't want to go all the way.

"When my daughter was nine years old, she wanted to be an astronaut," says Norma, a corporate attorney from Chicago. "By the time she was eleven, she wouldn't get off the couch because she didn't want to chip her nails. What happened?"

Being a girl has never been easy. Despite significant changes in the status of women and girls in the last century, a girl faces new and difficult challenges in an increasingly complex world. She also confronts many of the obstacles you may remember from girlhood, including conflicting messages and definitions about what it means to be female.

Think back to when you were a girl. Do you remember what you were told? Do you remember what you saw?

When you were a girl, were your ideas heard and valued? Did anyone talk with you openly and honestly about your body, about sex, about love?

What kind of encouragement did you get for pursuing your goals? Did this encouragement come with practical advice and support? Did the people who raised you expect you to achieve great things, or did they expect you to marry someone who would do that for you?

Did you ever imagine you would one day have your own daughter?

The way you are raising and mentoring the girl in your life relates directly to how you were treated as a girl. As a child of your generation and as your own mother's daughter, you bring a rich and complicated set of expectations and emotions to your role as her parent or guide. This book will help you recognize the impact of your own girlhood in shaping your approach to mothering a girl. It will also provide you with practical tools for helping a girl to be her own best advocate by knowing and asserting her rights, and becoming strong, smart, and bold in every aspect of her life.

Anyone who engages in a respectful and supportive relationship with a girl is invited to participate fully in her empowerment. Take this opportunity to envision your role as that of an "othermother." A girl needs many adults in her life on whom she can rely for encouragement and guidance, as well as for listening, loving, and bearing witness to her personal growth and achievement.

The girl you cherish, interact with most often, and with whom you have the greatest impact may not be your own daughter. She may be a student, a niece, a sister, a granddaughter, or the daughter of a friend. Because you play an essential role in a girl's life, this book—its message of empowerment and its call to action on a girl's behalf—is also for you.

Girls Incorporated

Starting very early on, a girl is repeatedly rewarded for being polite, behaving well, and looking pretty, while a boy is rewarded for making things, completing projects, and winning. A girl who learns to value and derive self-worth from superficial attributes grows into a woman who has not mastered the skills she needs to be confident, self-sufficient, and powerful.

Girls Incorporated, the leading advocacy organization for

girls in the United States, is trying to change all this. Since 1945, it has been preparing girls to lead successful, independent, and fulfilling lives through its innovative programs, cutting-edge research, and openness to take on issues that have a direct impact on a girl's world.

Girls Inc. believes that every one of the 36 million girls in this country has the right to be valued and respected at home, at school, and in her community. Its Girls' Bill of Rights affirms that:

- **Girls have the right** to be themselves and to resist gender stereotypes.
- **Girls have the right** to express themselves with originality and enthusiasm.
- **Girls have the right** to take risks, to strive freely, and to take pride in success.
- **Girls have the right** to accept and appreciate their bodies.
- **Girls have the right** to have confidence in themselves and to be safe in the world.
- **Girls have the right** to prepare for interesting work and economic independence.

"In order for a girl to navigate her way through barriers, she must be given the emotional, physical, and intellectual skills to assert herself," says Isabel Carter Stewart, former president of Girls Inc. "A girl should be inspired to get past whatever blocks her way—to create another opening, a better way in—instead of standing outside and railing about the injustice of being shut out."

Girls are experiencing more pressure now than ever before, according to a national Girls' Rights Survey conducted by Harris Interactive for Girls Inc. in 1999. Two thousand girls and boys in grades three through twelve were asked to say what rights girls have and don't have and how those rights shape girls' lives today and their hopes for the future. Even though today's girls are confident and ambitious, the vast majority say they are frustrated by outdated stereotypes that stand in their way. They also feel pressure to conform to narrow and often conflicting expectations imposed on them, restrictions that the girls say only become more limiting and defined as they get older.

"The message that girls are receiving?" asks Heather Johnston Nicholson, Ph.D., director of research at Girls Inc. "Sure, go ahead and study to be a brain surgeon. But first, be sure the chores are done, look pretty and thin, keep your voice down, and make everyone around you happy."

Women understand well the challenges that girls face. More than two-thirds of women in the Girls' Rights Survey say they believe that life is more difficult for girls today than when they were young, and that gender stereotypes not only exist but also are harmful to girls.

"It scares me to see how much pressure my nine-year-old daughter is feeling," says Kate, a stay-at-home mother from suburban Dallas. "She's worried all the time about her weight, her popularity with boys, her grades. All her role models are from the teen magazines and television shows, and she constantly compares herself with them. Not surprisingly, she always comes up short."

Even though children learn about values, money, sexuality,

body image, and so on, from many sources, research from Girls Inc. clearly identifies parents—especially mothers—as the primary educators of their children. Most girls say that it is their mother whose advice they seek and value, the one they look to for guidance and direction.

"I want to talk to my mom like I always have," says Jessica, an eighth grader from New York. "I want to be able to tell her the truth about what I'm doing and thinking without her getting mad or nervous."

According to Dr. Nicholson, in order to be an "askable person," the first one your daughter can turn to for answers, primarily about issue-laden topics, you must first create a safe, nonjudgmental environment in your home where she feels free to ask those difficult questions.

"The best way to communicate with your daughter," Dr. Nicholson advises, "is to tell her what she wants to know."

"Your Inner Girl"

How did you learn about your rights when you were a girl? Did it occur to you that you had the right to express yourself and move about freely and safely in your environment? To enjoy your femininity and prepare for a fulfilling career? To aspire for greatness and recognition?

Activities developed by Girls Inc. are included in each chapter as a way of helping you to connect with your daughter or a girl you care about and understand her world. These activities are a jumping-off point for starting a conversation and keeping it going. They also focus on your own experiences of being a girl and give you a perspective on how far you have come from the girl you once were.

As you begin to see your childhood as distinctly separate from that of the girl in your life, you will find it easier to give her a separate space to deal with the problems, desires, and conflicts that are part of growing up. By reflecting on what you went through when you were her age, you will discover common points of reference that will help strengthen your relationship with her and support her efforts to stand up for her rights.

You may unearth a few gems from your past, some wisdom handed down to you from another time and place, that you can use as you build an important and lasting connection with a girl—one that will inspire her to act with passion and intention throughout her life. You may also discover feelings of resentment or disappointment in the face of negative messages you may have received as a girl. Being ambitious, opinionated, sexual, or smart may not have been welcomed or dealt with appropriately by the people who raised you. You may feel anger at your own parents and at society for not providing you with enough support, or for failing to keep you safe from harm. This is your chance to deal with those feelings and refocus on creating a healthy and empowering environment for your own daughter and other girls you care about.

Your basic understanding of the developmental strengths and needs of girls will serve as an important guide as you read this book. The qualities you observe in a girl—the conflicts she may be facing, a desire for more closeness with you, a greater need for independence—all signal the ways in which she is growing up.

"Sometimes I feel as if I entered a world where I don't know what's up or down," says Patricia, an administrative assistant in a large San Francisco law firm. "My fifteen-year-old daughter's life is changing so fast—I don't know if either one of us can keep up with it."

It is an exciting journey to explore a girl's world together with your own. You will see how you each express yourself, learn what is important to you both, discover what the other thinks and cares about, and share how the two of you feel about her growing up.

Like any girl today, you too have the right to be confident in making strong, smart, and bold decisions. You have the right to appreciate your body, take risks, and make mistakes as you discover strengths you may never have known you had. This book will offer you the support and encouragement you deserve as you challenge your own and society's expectations of what a girl is and should be.

You are not alone in dealing with the complex issues involved with raising a girl in today's society. Remember, the girl in your life is the most important expert: trust her by giving her a voice and help her to maintain that voice. She is your best ally in helping her grow up to be a confident, courageous, and caring woman.

1.

Resisting Gender Stereotypes

*"Just be proud of your gender. There
is no shame in being yourself."*
TIFFANY, AGE SIXTEEN

I want a bike for my birthday, Mom." A simple enough request, or so Janet thought. Her daughter was turning six and was ready for a two-wheeler. Together, they drove to the toy store at the mall to find one suitable for her physically active daughter. Janet could still remember her own beloved first bicycle—jet black with shiny silver handlebars.

The salesperson led them to the bicycle section. "The girls' bikes are in the pink aisle, the boys' are in the blue," she explained.

> ## Girls' Bill of Rights #1
>
> Girls have the
> right to be
> themselves and
> to resist gender
> stereotypes.

Janet looked at pink bicycles decorated with bunnies and purple bikes covered with baby lambs. She saw bright yellow pom-poms hanging from handlebars painted cottony white. Curious, she checked out the boys' section. The bikes there were plain and solid: they looked clearly designed to hold up under strenuous use and hard play.

"What about one of these?" Janet asked her daughter.

"No way, Mom," she answered. "I want a pretty bike, like the one Nancy has."

Gender stereotypes are not just about toys and games. From the moment of birth, society treats boys and girls as if they were separate species. A girl is encouraged to be helpful, considerate, and caring; a boy to be tough, competitive, and strong. Sweating and physical exertion, considered unattractive for a girl but manly for a boy, affect the types of games they "should" play—or the bikes they buy. Gender-based discrimination not only shapes opportunities and experiences for boys and girls but also affects the way they see themselves, each other, and their world.

"Leveling the playing field is not just opening more doors for girls and giving equal treatment to girls and boys," says Jan Roberta, senior adviser for institutional advancement for Girls Inc. "It's *transforming* the way we look at gender as it relates to girls' and boys' development. Barriers and discrimination based on gender directly affect a girl's ability to participate more fully in our society."

The messages that most of us receive and too many of us pass on to girls is that boys and girls think differently, like to do different things, and have different abilities. Girls are nurturing; boys are aggressive. Boys need the lion's share of resources to grow healthy and strong and to develop into good providers and productive members of society; girls need less because they get into less trouble (except for teen pregnancy). Even if a girl pursues a career, it will be secondary to that of her husband and to her role as a mother and wife.

"A girl who learns that football is a boy's game won't sign up for a coed team, especially if she never had the opportunity to practice and develop skills in the sport," says Ms. Roberta. "A girl who is used to seeing adults pay more attention to boys will usually wait for things to quiet down or a boy to finish before speaking up herself. On the other hand, a boy who thinks cooking is for girls most likely won't venture into a class on nutrition, although he would probably love to take a survival class on campfire cooking."

Growing up in a male-dominated culture, many girls face tremendous pressures to conform to damaging notions of femininity that promote passivity and self-sacrifice. A girl learns early on to judge her self-worth according to narrow standards of physical attractiveness and to put the needs of others before her own. As a result, a recent Commonwealth Fund study found that girls are twice as likely as boys to suffer from depression.

"Adolescence is when girls experience social pressure to put aside their authentic selves and to display only a small portion of their gifts," writes Mary Pipher in *Reviving Ophelia*. "This pressure disorients and depresses most girls because they sense the pressure to be someone they are not."

A girl needs to know her rights, not her role. To that end, a girl needs to know herself. In addition, she must live in an environment that doesn't restrict her because she is female, but respects her for who she is and values her for what she can contribute to society.

Sixty percent of girls in the Girls' Rights Survey said they experience gender stereotypes that limit their right to be themselves. An empowered girl can challenge these limitations and reverse these stereotypes by understanding and exercising her rights, and advocating for the rights of others.

Getting to Know You

The following activities are a good starting point for exploring some of the feelings you experienced when you were growing up: to recall how you felt about the "right" to be yourself, not just who others wanted or expected you to be. By remembering your dreams and aspirations, you can encourage a girl to dream her own dreams and live out her own aspirations.

As you go along, you may find it helpful to jot down some of your thoughts and memories to read over at a later date or share with your daughter or the girl you care about at an appropriate time.

Advice

1. What is the best advice you ever got from your mother or another important adult in your life when you were growing up?
2. What is the worst advice you ever got?
3. What is the best advice you can give to a girl?

Expectations

Complete the following sentence fragments based on what you learned when you were a girl:

1. Girls are supposed to _____
2. Girls are not supposed to _____
3. Boys are supposed to _____
4. Boys are not supposed to_____ _____

The following exercise involves both you and the girl in your life. It will help you better understand what she is thinking about and how she regards you. It will also give her an insight into some of your feelings and emotions.

Mother/Daughter Portraits

Each of you is going to create a portrait of the other.

You will need a large sheet of paper and a marker to do this exercise.

1. Draw a large human figure, like the one shown on the next page.

2. At the top of the head, write *What does she think/dream about?*

3. At the place where a mouth would be, write *What does she talk about/say to me?*

4. At the places where the hands are, on the right hand, write *What does she spend her money on?* On the left hand, write *How does she spend her time?*

5. At the place over the heart, write *What does she care about?*

6. At the place over the belly, write *What does she worry about?*

7. At the base of the portrait, where the feet would be, write *What does she stand for/believe in?*

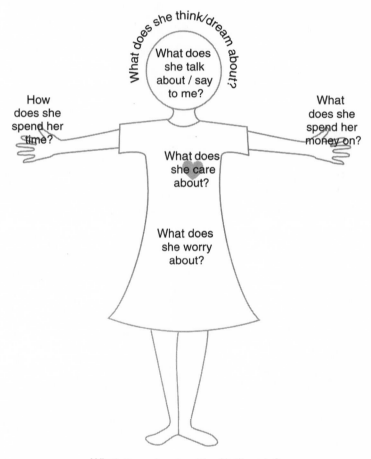

What does she stand for / believe in?

Next, write down at the corresponding place on the portrait a few words that you think best describe the other person. Feel free to use drawings or pictures as well. You may even want to decorate your portrait with stickers, colors, detailed features, and clothing. Be creative, but make sure that you also answer each question directly.

Keep in mind that this is not a visual representation of the person you (think you) know. It is a portrait of a person who dreams, cares, worries, spends, and believes in something.

Limit yourself to twenty minutes to complete this activity. Space yourself far enough away from each other so that you can concentrate on what you're doing and answer the questions honestly.

When you are both finished, take turns showing one another the portraits. What did you learn about how the other person sees you? In what ways do you feel "known"—understood and appreciated—by the other person? Does anything in the portrait surprise you? How can the two of you use what you've learned in your relationship?

The purpose of this activity is to see and deal with each other as two distinct individuals, beyond the surface of your roles as mother, daughter, girl, woman. It is also an opportunity to compare your similarities and differences, and to learn to give one another the space to be unique.

Getting Beyond the "Yuck"

"We want a girl to get down, get messy, get dirty, and enjoy!" says Pat Loomes, executive director of Girls Inc. of Alameda

County, the San Francisco/Bay Area of California. "She should get beyond the 'yuck'—to be comfortable holding a snake or greasing a lock or having her clothes splattered by paint. At the same time, we want to capture a girl's imagination about being female. We want to cultivate her creative abilities and nourish her caring qualities. It would be dreadful if women were just strong, smart, and brittle: a girl should know that it's possible—and preferable—to be both nurturing and strong."

Stereotypes about women are so ingrained in the fabric of our society that we rarely take the time to step back and examine how we treat girls and what we expect from them. To demonstrate, conduct a survey of housekeeping responsibilities in your own home.

Family Roles and Responsibilities

1. How is power and responsibility distributed among all the people in the house? In other words, who is in charge of what?

2. How are the chores divided? Does your son mow the lawn while your daughter does the dishes? Does your daughter avoid taking out the garbage because she thinks it's "gross"? Does everyone participate in household maintenance?

3. Who makes the rules? Enforces the rules? Does one person always sit at the head of the table? Who?

If any of the roles and responsibilities in your household are defined along gender lines, here is your opportunity to shake things up. Be sure to make chores and expectations flexible enough to accommodate personal choices, and changing interests and abilities. It should be acceptable for any member of the family to say: "I don't mind taking out the garbage, but I also want to learn how to cook"; "I don't like doing the dishes, so I would rather mow the lawn"; "I want to sit at the head of the table sometimes"; and so on.

Family roles and rules all work to reinforce a girl's ideas about her place in any relationship or group setting. If a girl's role is to be the sweet and delicate one who needs protecting at home, she is likely to believe she needs a lot of protecting in the world outside and will probably have a hard time standing on her own. If her role is to be the moody, misbehaving one whom no one can trust, she is likely to believe that she is not responsible, and therefore, not *worthy* of being treated with respect or held to a high standard of performance and behavior; she has failed before she ever began.

Chores such as setting the table or shoveling the snow help children acquire such important skills as respecting and finishing a task, which translate into accepting more involved responsibilities as they get older. The way a girl relates to teachers, the teller at the bank, authority figures, friends, and, one day, her own family naturally and inevitably extends from how she was valued growing up and the "role" she played—or was asked to play—in her family and home.

Listening to Each Other

"I just want freedom and acceptance for who I am and what I do," says Marci, twelve, who is in her first year of middle school in Eugene, Oregon. "My father still treats me like I'm a baby. He calls me the same names he did when I was five and it embarrasses me. Also, my parents don't think I'm responsible. They won't let me get a dog because they say I can't—or wouldn't—take care of it. They don't even give me a chance. I think it's more that *they* don't want a dog and they're putting it on me.

"What I don't understand is why my parents trust me to baby-sit my three-year-old brother but not to go out alone with my friends. Sometimes I think they're real hypocrites. I used to talk to my mother a lot when I was younger but now I hardly tell her anything. That's because when I recently confided in her that I liked a boy in my class, she got real upset. She told me to stay away from boys and I said, no way! So now I don't tell her anything or just lie. And that makes me feel really bad."

Girls don't want to disappoint their mothers, according to Pat Loomes, who points out that in essay contests sponsored by her Girls Inc. affiliate, *99 percent of girls chose their mother as the person they most admire in their lives because of the advice they've been given by her.*

"You think your daughter is ignoring you when you're giving advice because she rolls her eyes or turns away when you're talking," she says. "The truth is that she's really listening to you closely. Kids develop a sense of self-worth when they're told that they're fine and good and strong. It's not enough for them to just feel good about themselves, however; they have to learn the skills to be the person they want to be. Tell your daughter that she's wonderful but give her the tools so she can keep working on it."

Sara Shandler writes in *Ophelia Speaks: Adolescent Girls Write about Their Search for Self* that girls are caught in the crossfire between where they should be and where they really are. The following activities will help you discover where a girl is now in her life and open up new avenues of communication between the two of you.

Reading Together

If you read together, bring new awareness to the reading. Ask her which characters she relates to in the books and stories she loves. Whom does she like, whom does she hate, and why? If the book were to be made into a movie and she could be anyone in it, which character would she choose to play?

Encourage her to explore characters other than the hero/ine. If the story was told from the "friend's" point of view, how might it be different? Is there anything about the "bad guy" that she finds interesting, likable, or funny? If there are animals in the story, ask her which one she feels is most like her, and why.

It might be fun to do this exercise as a field trip to the bookstore. Spend some time in the children's section looking at the books that appeal to her.

What's in a Name?

Help a girl create an acrostic using the letters of her name. Spell out her name vertically and have her complete each letter by identifying some of her best qualities or focusing on what she does and what she likes. (Think of the song "M-O-T-H-E-R: 'M' is for the many things she gave me. . . .")

Steer her responses away from how she looks, how well she behaves, or how pleasant or helpful she is—even if you know her to be lovely, good, and kind. Action words and verbs are always best!

Portrait Collage

Help a girl create a self-portrait collage that illustrates her likes, dislikes, worries, fears, wishes, goals, and the activities she enjoys doing most. Clip images and words out of magazines; attach photographs of friends, beloved family members, and cherished animals; go wild with stickers and various sparkly, colorful decorations.

Encourage her to put this portrait in her room or any-where it can serve as a reminder of how interesting and worth knowing she is.

"I try to talk to my daughters as openly as possible, although sometimes it feels as if I'm three separate mothers because of the differences in their ages," says Meagan, the mother of three girls, ages seven, nine, and eleven. "For example, when I dis-agree with my eleven-year-old about one of her friends, I try to express my opinion in a way that doesn't sound as if I'm judging her. The younger ones, on the other hand, really want to know what I think about their friends and take my impres-sions almost literally.

"My husband and I are both public school teachers in Boston, and we want our daughters to get a good education so they'll be able to be independent and self-sufficient. Above all,

I want my daughters to respect themselves, no matter what men think of them. I was brought up in a strict family where it was a man's world. Over the years, I've become less traditional, more sure of myself. Now, I'm more empowered and I try very hard to communicate that feeling to my daughters.

"When I was growing up, girls took ballet and played with other girls. Our goal was to meet a nice man. The flip side of all the pressure that kids are getting from the media today is that they're also learning there's a whole world of opportunity out there. I'm grateful for this barrage of information because I want my daughters to aim high and be strong by themselves, apart from me."

Parents should show the same respect to their children as they show to other adults, advises Jan Stanton, Girls Inc. director of program development. "Instead of judging what they are telling us, we should listen to what they're saying," she says. "Children must know that they have a voice and that their voice is heard and respected."

Girls Under the Hood

Cara, age seventeen, and her parents were preparing to visit her first-choice college for an admissions interview. It was a long trip and Cara was nervous about the state of the family car and whether it could make it to its destination without breaking down.

Her solution? Cara took the car to a nearby service station for a routine exam. The mechanic there checked the tire pressure and the fluid levels—tasks easily performed by someone with the most minor knowledge of automobile basics—proclaimed the car fit for the journey, and handed Cara a bill that came to $50 for his time and labor.

To many women, what lurks under the hood of an automobile is one of life's greatest mysteries. The automobile can be an extremely intimidating machine, especially for women who lack confidence in dealing with even the most minor maintenance or repairs such as changing a flat tire. It isn't that women lack the strength or ability to tackle these problems—it's just that historically most women haven't been given the opportunity to learn how to deal with these problems when they arise.

Cars are such a necessity in our daily lives that it becomes very important to give girls such as Cara an equal opportunity to learn to overcome their perception that automobile repair and maintenance are beyond their capabilities.

Girls Under the Hood, a program sponsored by Girls Inc. of Greater Atlanta in collaboration with Marietta Toyota, introduces a girl to the field of automobile mechanics starting when she is ten years old. At the same time that she is learning about basic automobile technology, maintenance, and troubleshooting, she is being introduced to a career opportunity not usually presented to her (less than 10 percent of all mechanics are women). Not only does she gain confidence and self-esteem from acquiring new skills, she also saves money on basic do-it-yourself car repairs such as replacing wipers, fixing flat tires, changing the oil, and so on.

According to Rich Tymer of Toyota's Technical Education Network, there is a strong need for trained mechanics with the intelligence to diagnose and prescribe the correct repair for automobiles, especially now that cars have as many as ten computers incorporated in their systems.

"I believe that women mechanics will bring a new level of diagnostic achievement to the industry," he says, "along with a new level of trust with consumers."

Girls Under the Hood is an important example of breaking down the stereotypes imposed on girls and making these false notions obsolete. The program is an important model in that it teaches a girl that intelligent problem solving, not muscle strength, is the major requirement in automobile repair. It also puts a girl in an environment where she performs a nontraditional role and may awaken her interest in other fields that previously seemed out of reach, such as aerospace technology or computer science.

As an extra benefit, a girl garners a high level of respect from other girls as well as members of the opposite sex because she is looked up to for her courage to enter a field historically dominated by men.

Learning Together

The following activities are just some examples of how you and a girl can acquire practical new skills together that challenge gender stereotyping.

1. Re-create Girls Under the Hood in your own driveway by learning about the basic maintenance and repair of your family car. Ask a person who knows about automobiles to give both of you pointers on how to fix a flat tire, measure the oil, refill wiper fluid, and so on.

2. Study the stock market together. Read the financial section of the newspaper out loud, and discuss interest rates, investment strategies, and personal and family budgets.

3. Fix things around the house. Most women learn how to make basic household repairs if they are single or after they are divorced or widowed. These skills should be learned not out of necessity, but for basic self-sufficiency.

4. Work on the computer together. Explore the Internet, create a Web page, find mother–daughter pen pals from another country and start an e-mail correspondence with them.

Traditionally, a boy is given more opportunities than a girl to become interested in such occupations as automobile mechanic, television technician, mechanical engineer, draftsperson, landscaper, electrician, and aircraft mechanic, to name a few. Programs such as Girls Under the Hood change the perceptions that limit a girl's career path by giving her the chance to explore nontraditional activities and possible vocations, as well as helping her learn practical survival skills for everyday living.

Gender Equity

Gender stereotyping is alive and well in the year 2000, according to the Girls' Rights Survey, even though 86 percent of all girls rate the right to be themselves and resist pressure to behave in sex-stereotyped ways as very important.

"Girls are still thought of as weak, sexy, emotional, and brainless," explains Dr. Heather Johnston Nicholson. "Yet, paradoxically, as girls become 'tougher,' more outspoken, and opinionated, there's more of a societal pressure to conform. In my day, all the building blocks we played with were the same brownish, reddish color. Now there are pink building blocks for girls and blue ones for boys: a girl is instructed how to construct her dream house or a shopping mall; a boy is taught to erect a fortress or factory."

Equity today goes far beyond the legally conceived notions of equal opportunity. In her book *Mathematics and Gender*, the educator Elizabeth Fennema distinguishes between the three levels of equity:

1. Equity of Access—the equal opportunity for girls and boys to participate in programs and activities. Access, however, is more than just being careful not to exclude girls and young women. The subtle and overt messages that invite and encourage girls or keep them away must also be considered: how welcoming or hostile different environments are for girls; what opportunities are offered them; and how girls are recruited.

2. Equity of Treatment—the same level and quality of attention and resource given to girls and boys. Some considerations include if girls are called on as much boys; if they have the same opportunity and support to become interested and skilled in nontraditional areas and in athletics.

3. Equity of Outcome—the actual measurement of changes in the gap between females and males in achievement, knowledge, confidence, persistence, and participation. When

gender barriers and limitations have been eliminated, changes should be seen among boys as well as girls. For example, more girls will be able to repair their own bikes and more boys will know how to mend their clothing.

"Girls are ready to create change—to cast out timeworn stereotypes about who girls are and what girls can do," says Dr. Nicholson. "Suppose you know a girl who wants to grow up to run her own construction company and bid successfully on those lucrative highway jobs. You would want her grandfather to buy her a shiny yellow bulldozer toy to play with when she is two or three years old; her aunt to give her a construction software package for her computer when she is nine or ten; her middle school basketball coach to tell her she has guts and to work with her on plotting set plays for the team; and her high school counselor to encourage her to take the tough college prep math courses and seek early admission and a scholarship to an engineering program in a good university.

"In short, you would want her to encounter high expectations, unlimited opportunities, and adults who support her highest aims. Yet the reality for today's girl is that she is expected to plan for a demanding career, help around the house, look attractive, and stay quiet and demure. This all sounds pretty daunting if your dreams include state highway contracts and your precalculus homework is due!"

According to an international study published in 1999 in the journal *Sex Roles*, the stereotypes most associated with women are "feminine," "affectionate," "emotional," "superstitious," "attractive," "sensitive," and "sexy." The stereotypes most associated with men are "masculine," "adventurous," "forceful," "strong," "tough," and "coarse." In every country surveyed, the female stereotype is weaker and less active than the male stereotype.

The Girls' Rights Survey found that girls who have adult support are more resilient and likely to overcome the negative effects of gender stereotypes. While nine out of ten girls say they know three adults to whom they could go if they had a problem, girls who had a poor quality of life (i.e., not many friends, trouble getting along with their parents, problems at school, and so on) are ten times more likely to say they do not have an adult support system as girls with a high quality of life.

"With the help of adults, girls must continue to resist, debunk, and overcome the limitations imposed on them by our society," insists Dr. Nicholson.

Elena is a pediatrician in Tucson who treats low-income families at a community clinic. She is also the mother of a daughter who is ten and a son who is eight.

"I'm finding to my surprise that there's a big difference between raising a boy and a girl," she says. "Even though my daughter loves gymnastics, soccer, and horseback riding, my son is much more physical in the way he plays, how he interacts, even how he expresses himself. I have the same expectations for both my son and daughter, but I find myself making a special effort to make sure I don't give my daughter any reason to doubt herself. I also want her to have as many opportunities as possible to explore her interests.

"I'm the youngest of five children—my oldest sister is fourteen years older than I am. I've always had very strong female role models and was never told I couldn't do something because I was female. I'm passing on this belief in a woman's worth on to my daughter because I want her to be self-assured and confident in her abilities.

"I find it so exciting to watch my daughter develop into her own person. She's beginning to express her own style in the way she dresses and how she wears her hair. She's still young enough that I usually win if there's a disagreement, and I know I should enjoy this time as long as I can. Adolescence is right around the corner and I figure I won't be winning many arguments then!

"I want my daughter to grow up to be her own person, to know that she doesn't need a boyfriend to be complete. There is so much more emphasis on boy-girl relationships at an earlier age than when I was growing up. Already in my daughter's fourth-grade class, there is a lot of teasing about who is someone's boyfriend or girlfriend. My daughter was so stressed out on Valentine's Day because she was worried she wouldn't get a lot of cards and that the boys she sent cards to would get the wrong message about how she felt about them.

"My daughter sees that the women around her are all very strong in different ways, and this sets an example for her. I want her to know that if she ever has a problem or is uncomfortable with something, she can come to me—I still go to my mom for advice. But if my daughter ever feels she can't talk for some reason or another, I know there are other women she trusts and can turn to for help and advice—this makes me feel happy and very fortunate."

Girls and the Media

From June Cleaver, who effortlessly managed an immaculate home, to the blond bombshells who patrolled the beaches on *Baywatch,* girls have turned on their televisions and tuned in to unachievable standards of female perfection. Women are often seen as perfect homemakers or as too-beautiful-to-be-true sex symbols. Real women who juggle work, family, and finances are too often absent from the screen. So are real girls who try to make sense of school, friends, and puberty, and struggle against complex pressures.

Magazines and advertising also have a huge impact on the way girls and women think of themselves. In her book *Deadly Persuasion: Why Women and Girls Need to Fight the Addictive Power of Advertising,* Jean Kilbourne documents how advertisements that target girls encourages them to be thinner, quieter, nicer, more passive, more approval-seeking, more beautiful, sexier, and virginal.

In addition, teenage girls care very much about what other people think of them compared to teenage boys, according to research conducted at the University of New Hampshire. The 1999 study found that this "emotional reliance" on others is associated with higher rates of depression.

"There's an incredible pressure to be like everyone else," says Shawna, a fourteen-year-old from Columbus, Ohio. "I try to feel confident but when I look at television or read one of the teen magazines, I feel so different. My family is nothing like those on the TV programs, and my bedroom—which I share with my older sister—can never be as cool as the ones they show in the magazines. Sometimes I feel like a real loser."

The following activity will give you a better insight into how the media affect a girl's view of herself and other girls and women.

Media Messages: Reality Rating

A girl sees images of women on television, on billboards, in newspapers, commercials, comic books, and magazines. What does she think of them? Does she ever comment on these images? Do you?

1. Gather some old magazines, newspapers, and advertisements that feature images of women.

2. Set aside some time to look at these images together. Ask a girl what she thinks of this one or that one. Which ones look most like the women in her life—her teachers, her friends, the mothers of her friends? Which ones does she think are fine; which are somewhat interesting or cool; which are just plain gross—and why?

3. Think about how these images make you feel as a grown woman and as a person who has already survived adolescence. Share your opinions with her as well. Be sure to tell her what you think, rather than what you believe she should think. You will learn far more about a girl by letting her say what's really on her mind, even if it makes you uncomfortable.

Use this activity to discuss the messages the media sends about how a woman should look and act, compared to what a girl experiences in her own life. Talk about television programs, movies, magazines, and advertisements that do a good job of realistically portraying girls and women, and help a girl distinguish between what the media considers "ideal" and the reality of her own world.

Girls Re-Cast TV

Television has a huge influence on the lives of young people; on average, they watch about twenty-one hours of TV a week and most watch it every day. "Re-Casting TV: Girls' Views," a 1996 Girls Inc. survey of more than 2,000 boys and girls in grades three through twelve from schools across the country, found that 99 percent of American households have a television set; 85 percent of homes contain a VCR (96 percent in homes with children); 65 percent of households have cable television; 58 percent of children say they have a television set in their bedroom; and more girls than boys say they watch television every day (64 percent versus 58 percent).

Think About: How old were you when you first started watching TV? What were your favorite shows then and what are they now, and why? Do you watch television alone or with your family? Who's in charge of deciding what programs to watch?

The images on television are different from the lives of most girls. Thirty-nine percent of the girls in the survey say that their world—their family, friends, the people in their neighborhood, the kinds of things they like to do, and the problems they face—is "hardly ever" or "never" portrayed on television. In the real world, 80 percent of single households are headed by women; on sitcoms, half of the single parent households are headed by men.

Although 13 percent of the people in the United States are poor, only 1 percent of the people on television are poor. In addition, most girls think there are too few television programs that teach kids how to deal with real-life pressures like sex, divorce, violence, or abuse at home.

Reality Quiz: Together with your daughter, compare your family to one portrayed on television. Figure out what's similar and what's different. For example, in your life and TV life, who lives together as a family? Where do they live? A house? An apartment? Who works outside the home? What are their jobs? What do the kids and/or parents talk about? Fight about? What do they spend their money on? What's important to the children? The parents?

More than half of the girls in the "Re-Casting TV" survey say they have watched something on television that has upset them or made them angry, including news items, violence-related programs, or shows about racism and prejudice. Girls want to see characters who look like them, who share their aspirations and fears, and who deal realistically with the issues they face every day. They also want television to show more racial and ethnic diversity, more adventures for girls, and more programs with a message.

Parents and children disagree about how often they talk to one another about what kids see on television. Parents are nearly five times as likely to say they talk to their children about the programs their kids watch on television as kids are to say that they talk to their parents. The majority of parents say they make the decision as to what to watch on television when they are watching with their children. In contrast, only 26 percent of children say these decisions are made by the parents.

Look, Listen, and Ask: Watch some of a girl's favorite television programs with her. Afterward, ask her if the girls and women on TV look like her or anyone she knows. Do they behave like her and her friends? Do the women in her favorite shows work outside the home? What kind of jobs do they have? Does she know anyone who has this kind of job?

Ask her how the characters talk about things that she talks about with her friends and family. Can she imagine herself talking like her favorite character on television? How is she different from her or him? How is she similar? Help her to write some lines that she would want her favorite character to say.

A girl should have the opportunity to evaluate what she sees and hears on television, and understand that the stereotypes depicted on the screen do not always reflect what she experiences in her life. It is important to know how a girl views the way girls and women are portrayed in the media so you can better understand some of the pressures she faces on a daily basis.

Endless Opportunity

"We believe in endless opportunity," says Pat Loomes of Girls Inc. "I've seen girls start out majoring in engineering or physics and then switch over to ethnic studies or psychology. Why? Is this what they really want? Or were they put down by their professor? Discouraged by their adviser? Were they the only girl in their class and made to feel uncomfortable and 'weird'?

"Let's get rid of the hand wringing and encourage a girl to expand her range of possibilities instead. Let's help a girl to be heart surgeon as well as a pediatrician, a mechanic as well as a teacher. Our job is to help a girl set higher expectations for herself while giving her the tools to accomplish her dreams."

It is an exciting time to be a girl and to raise a girl. To feel honored and valued for who she is, a girl must know that she is entitled to equal treatment in all aspects of her life and be inspired to take pride in her true self.

Ways to Empower a Girl to Be Herself

• *Praise a girl for her skills and success, not only for her appearance. Say "You did a terrific job," instead of "You look pretty today."*

• *Ask a girl if she wants a truck, a doll, a jewelry box, a chemistry set, a flute, a bass drum, a new dress, some new software, etc. Keep her options open.*

• *Make sure that household chores such as caring for younger children, cleaning up, preparing meals, cutting the grass, taking out the garbage, fixing things, etc., are shared equally by girls, boys, men, and women in your home.*

- *Try some role reversal at home. Let a girl sit at the head of the table and a boy prepare his favorite meal for the whole family.*

- *Watch your language. Get "boys will be boys" and "you know how girls are" out of your vocabulary.*

- *Help a girl get beyond the "yuck." If the opportunity presents itself, insist calmly that she hold a snake, play in the mud, and get her hands dirty discovering the world around her.*

- *Introduce a girl to dynamic women and men who combine paid work, volunteer work, and family life in innovative ways.*

- *Celebrate the accomplishments of women throughout history.*

- *Read a girl's textbooks: Are women's contributions included in history, science, and art? If not, talk to the board of education and/or create a committee for change.*

- *Confront the widespread notions of female fragility by challenging the view in the media and elsewhere of assertive women as "unfeminine" or destructive.*

- *Teach a girl to watch television and movies with a critical eye, discuss what you've seen together, and look for strong, smart women who are not limited to traditional roles.*

- *Ask questions and take action if you see something unfair or biased on television. Write a letter to your local station or the producers of the show voicing your objections.*

- *Be aware of what a girl is reading and responding to in media and advertising. If she is drawn to sexist stereotypes, ask what appeals to her. Find a way to share your views without judging hers.*

- *Write letters to toy and publishing companies that produce toys, books, and materials you feel promote stereotypes about gender.*

- *Address sexism in areas where young people are sorted by gender into educational or sports programs based on interests or skills they are "supposed" to have.*

- *Work with other parents and teachers to foster nonsexist environments from nursery school on up.*

2.

Speaking Freely and Openly

"Every girl has dreams and good ideas, but if she doesn't tell them to anyone, how are they ever going to come true?"
—ANNA, AGE TEN

Every woman should have a room of her own, a place where she can discover her true voice and explore her innermost thoughts and feelings. Before she goes out into the world, before she attempts to change, improve, or relate to her world, a woman must know her own voice and feel free to express it honestly.

Does your daughter or the girl you care about have a room of her own? If so, would she agree to lead you on a tour?

The room may be a literal one: her bedroom or a section of the bedroom. Or it may be symbolic. For instance, a girl may decorate her locker at school, write all over her backpack and notebook covers, or create poetry, art, and music. In any case, she has probably carved out some space

> *Girls' Bill of Rights #2*
>
> Girls have the right to express themselves with originality and enthusiasm.

where she feels free to express herself in the ways that appeal to her talents and sensibilities.

By visiting a girl's room—literal or symbolic—you can observe the many ways in which she is already expressing herself with originality and enthusiasm. And, as you tune in to the many signals a girl is sending out, you become a stronger ally for her as she discovers her voice and claims her right to express herself honestly at home, at school, in her community, and in her relationships.

Does your daughter or a girl you care about share her room with another sibling? Is she free to decorate however she wants? Take this opportunity to encourage her to claim one place in the house—even a corner of a room—as her very own.

A Room of Her Own

1. Ask your daughter to lead you on a field trip to her room. Pretend that you are seeing it for the first time. Ask her to point things out as though you never saw them before. Ask her to describe the significance of certain objects—for example, posters, trinkets, trophies.

2. Observe the colors; notice what is thrown around and what is organized neatly; look at the photos in their frames; notice what music she listens to, what books and magazines she is reading. Does she have a distinctive style?

3. Step back and take in the whole picture. What does she feature prominently, and what is presumably in the drawers, in the closet, under the bed, or put away? Keep in

mind, it is up to her to lead this tour—to show or not show what she wants. What is she expressing indirectly through her room?

4. Consider how your daughter or the girl in your life responds to this activity. Does she want to prepare her room first, get everything arranged a certain way before you enter, or does she just say, "Sure, come on in"? She may not want to do this activity at all, in which case it's best to honor her decision.

This activity is not necessarily an occasion to comment on how a girl chooses to live. For example, statements like: "Wow—you sure are secretive [boy-crazed, a neat freak, a slob]" do not build trust. It may not be useful for you to share your judgments or your more critical insights and opinions. Choose what you say with care. Some impressions you will just want to take in and let be.

Letting a girl know that you have seen her, and that you are paying attention to who she is, is the first step toward drawing out her truest self and her authentic voice. The most important gift you can give the girl you care for now is space to express herself in healthy and creative ways.

The following activity will help you to start thinking about your earliest attempts to express yourself as a girl.

Let's Talk About You

• *Name-calling: Were you ever called a loudmouth? Or, conversely, were you ever ridiculed for being too shy?*

- *Public speaking: Do you remember the first time you spoke up in a room full of adults and/or other children? What happened?*

- *The look says it all: What is the weirdest thing you ever wore and/or did to your hair as a teenager or young girl? How did your parents respond to your clothing and hair-dos?*

Have you ever shared these stories with the girl in your life? If not, tell her what it was like for you to speak up for yourself when you were her age.

Breaking the Code of Silence

Rose is a thirteen-year-old from central Alabama. Recently, her friends were talking about another girl in school, calling the girl a "slut" and "trash." Rose told them she thought it was wrong to talk about someone like that, and her friends responded to her comments by ignoring her for a whole week. Now, when one of her friends says something she doesn't like, Rose feels her face getting hot, but says nothing out loud. She has decided it's probably better to keep her mouth closed and her opinions to herself.

Better to keep quiet. Better not to make trouble. These are some of the most damaging messages a girl can get. In *Reviving Ophelia*, Mary Pipher describes the enormous pressure on girls to deny their true selves in order to please the people around them. In early adolescence, she explains, girls are expected to sacrifice the so-called "masculine" parts of themselves that our culture finds so threatening in girls and women. At this stage, girls are discouraged from expressing themselves honestly and directly since they risk hurting other people's feelings or coming off as arrogant, confrontational, argumentative, or merely difficult.

"This is when girls learn to be nice rather than honest," writes Dr. Pipher.

According to the Girls' Rights Survey, 56 percent of girls say it's true that "girls are expected to speak softly and not cause trouble." As girls get older, they are even more likely to agree with this statement and the majority say they don't like it at all.

"How come every time a girl makes a formal speech in front of a crowd, someone has to stand up and make a big joke about it after she's finished?" asks Caroline, age eighteen. She describes how she spent most of her girlhood in Houston trying to be as quiet as possible in all situations—especially school.

"I hated speaking up in class," she explains, "because I was scared that the other kids would laugh at me or think I was stupid. I never argued for my opinions and I cowered at my desk unless the teacher asked me a direct question. I was so afraid of saying something wrong and not being perfect."

More than half the girls in the Girls' Rights Survey say they experience stereotypes that limit their right to express themselves with originality and enthusiasm. In addition, a study conducted by the Horatio Alger Association found that approximately one in three girls do not feel they have the "opportunity for open discussion in their classes."

The pressure on girls to say something nice or say nothing at all comes from all sides—schools, parents, religious institutions, magazines, music, television, advertising, and movies. According to Mary Pipher, this pressure is especially powerful and upsetting for girls when it comes from their peers.

"Girls face two choices," she explains. "They can be true to themselves and risk abandonment by their peers, or they can reject their true selves and fit in. Since self-esteem is based on the ability to accept one's thoughts and feelings as one's own, a girl suffers enormous losses if she distances herself from her ideas in order to gain approval or maintain close relationships."

Laura, a nurse in a small town in New Jersey, describes her distress when her fifteen-year-old daughter began dressing like Marilyn Manson, an androgynous but heavily made-up male musician and powerful voice among many young people.

"My daughter wore black clothes and heavy eyeliner to school every day," she says. "We had grand fights about it, because I didn't like it. Ultimately, she gave up this look in response to pressure from her classmates who began treating her like an outcast. It didn't seem to matter to her at all what I thought."

Even a seemingly superficial preference, such as the clothes and colors one chooses to wear, can mark a girl as undesirable and unacceptable among her peers. "They expect you to be the same every day," says Susanna, a twelve-year-old from Cleveland, Ohio. "I bought a new outfit that I liked and people at school made fun of me for wearing it. So now it's just hanging in my closet."

While clothes are one way that a girl may stifle a part of

herself in order to win friends, this pressure to conform inevitably extends into deeper aspects of a girl's personality. Soon her values and her judgment become subject to her friends' approval.

"It's hardly tragic if the clothes go back into the closet when people disapprove," says Jan Stanton, director of program development at Girls Inc. "But if the feelings that inspire a girl to present herself a certain way end up in the closet along with the discarded outfits, she's going to suffer. A girl who hides her true self behind a closed door risks becoming so out of touch with her real feelings and opinions that she will never know how interesting and exciting she really is—and neither will anyone else."

Giving Voice to Values

Eleven-year-old Chris and her sister, Allie, age eight, live in Sioux City, Iowa. They have an uncle they both love very much who has been open with the family for many years about being gay. All their lives, Chris and Allie have heard that being gay is natural and "no big deal." But one week in church, the preacher gave an entire sermon saying that homosexuality is wrong. He said it is okay to "love the sinner," but being gay is still a sin. Now Allie is worried. She doesn't want her uncle to be a sinner. And Chris is angry. She would like to ask the preacher how he can say those things about her uncle, when he never even met him.

Often the viewpoints of young girls are ignored, invalidated, or misunderstood. Girls Inc. former president Isabel Carter Stewart believes that as a society, we do not value the judgment of children. "We don't believe that girls and boys know what is good for them," she says. "In a way, we are reluctant to believe that they have values and that these values may be extremely meaningful to them."

Ms. Stewart adds that with a girl, there is the additional layer of gender discrimination and of gender stereotyping that fosters the notion that she is superficial and frivolous. "Girls— even very young girls—tell us how frustrating it is when people assume that all they are thinking about is how they look and whether they are attractive to boys," she says.

A girl should be encouraged to express her real identity and hold on to her values as a way to combat the intense pressure to be like everyone else.

"When girls lose their subjective fix on the universe, they are adrift and helpless, their self-esteem hostage to the whims of others," writes Mary Pipher. All girls experience pain at this point in their development, as a result of running smack into the judgments or criticisms of other people whose opinions matter greatly to them. "If that pain is blamed on themselves, it manifests itself as depression," she says. "If that pain is blamed on others—on parents, peers, or the culture—it shows up as anger."

Dr. Pipher attests to the fact that some girls may destroy their true selves in order to be socially acceptable, while others strive to become fully feminine and fail. Ironically, a girl who "successfully" adapts her personality to meet the expectations of others by dressing, talking, and thinking like the crowd, emerges from adolescence more dependent and lacking in coping skills than one who was socially isolated and lonely during puberty because she was different.

"Girls who survive adolescence the most intact have managed to hold on to some sense of their own specialness," Dr. Pipher writes. "Pride in their ethnic identity, being part of a community, having a talent, believing in a cause, or feeling genuinely useful to others provides the foundation for a strong sense of self and the courage to express oneself openly—no matter what anybody else thinks."

What do a girl's feelings about certain issues reveal about her beliefs, her values? Does she express strong opinions about what her friends or other people are doing? Does she take an interest in politics? How does she distinguish between right and wrong? The statements provided in the following activity will help you find out more about a girl's values and about how comfortable she feels (or does not feel) expressing them.

Values Voting

Encourage a girl to choose between the following responses: *agree, undecided,* or *disagree,* in reply to a list of statements expressing a range of values. For example, how does she respond to the statement "A woman should be married before she considers having a baby"? If she agrees with this statement, begin a conversation with her about it. What does she see as the advantages of being married when you have a child? What does a child need that a married mother can provide? What makes a good marriage?

This activity creates a safe space for a girl to explore and express what she really feels about a particular issue or idea without fearing that she will be ostracized, punished, or judged harshly for her views. These value statements also offer you an opportunity to initiate conversations about difficult topics, to find out what kind of information a girl is getting from the media and people closest to her, and to observe how she is processing that information.

Value Statements:

- Female athletes are not feminine.
- A woman is not complete until she has a baby.
- It's better to say what you really feel, even if it means hurting someone's feelings.
- Couples who fight are going to break up or get a divorce.
- People who cry when they're upset are more healthy than people who don't cry.
- You should always think before you speak.
- Men should not have to take responsibility for birth control—that's the woman's job.
- If there were more professional women's sports teams, they would probably have as many fans as the men's teams.
- Women should make as much money as men make for doing the same job.
- The president has to be a man, because women are not as strong in making decisions.

Did you learn anything that you did not already know about the girl in your life? Does she enjoy talking about her values? Does she appear to take pride in her beliefs?

Weave this activity into your lives by drawing on relevant examples from the culture to keep the conversations going. When your daughter or niece or mentee learned that a six-year-old girl was shot at school, how did she respond? What does she believe is the solution to the problem of violence in schools? It may seem too sophisticated or scary a topic for a very young girl, but if she has heard about the shooting, odds are she is thinking about it.

While doing this activity, be sure that you also share your values, even when your views are very different. Let a girl know what you think, let her know why, and then leave it at that.

Your goal should not be to change each others' minds, but rather to express a viewpoint and feel secure in your relationship, despite differences of opinion. This builds trust in open communication and helps you get to know one another better. More important, it gives a girl a safe place to practice expressing her feelings honestly, rather than bottling them up or deciding that they don't matter.

Dealing with Stress and Conflict—Out Loud

Making it okay for a girl to let it all out means making it safe for her to voice unpopular opinions, shout out wrong answers, and admit when she is overwhelmed. It is essential that the girl in your life feels free to share her worries and confusion with you, as well as all her brilliant ideas. The better you are able to handle the "real" her, the more inclined she will be to let you know when she is under a lot of stress and needs help coping. If you are approachable, a girl will feel more comfortable asking for your advice when she needs it, or asking you simply to listen to her before small problems turn into big ones.

"I want to be the kind of mother my daughter can talk to," says Deborah, a social worker from Indianapolis. Her daughter recently told her about a friend who got pregnant and then tried to induce a miscarriage by getting drunk and throwing herself down the stairs. "She was too ashamed and afraid to ask her mother for help," explains Deborah, who admits she would be extremely upset if her daughter got pregnant, "although I would rather she come to me with bad news than try to harm herself."

Girls, on the other hand, say that being open with their mothers is sometimes not an option—especially when discussing the rough stuff. "I asked my mom what a 'blow job' was," says Kendra, eleven, from Louisville, Kentucky, "and she freaked out. Then she grounded me for a week! I guess she thinks that teaches me a lesson but the reason I asked her in the first place was because I was kind of embarrassed to ask my friends—I was scared they would think I wasn't cool or something. It's not like I want to talk about bad words and sex with everybody I meet. I just want some information about something I don't know."

Girls describe dating without their parents knowing, lying about where they go, protecting friends who are involved in dangerous activities, and relying on friends (or the dictionary) anytime problems or questions arise.

Brenda Stegall is the director of training for Girls Inc. and has led workshops in cities all over the country to strengthen communication between mothers and daughters throughout adolescence. "Clashes between mothers and daughters, and fathers and daughters, are inevitable," she says. "Girls today have grown up in a world that is distinctly different from the one their parents remember. Their values may be different. Their stress is different. Greater opportunities for girls bring greater responsibility for *girls* and *their parents*. Both must be given the skills to talk and listen to one another when conflicts come up.

"If your daughter wants to talk to you about something that makes you uncomfortable or upset or completely mortified," Ms. Stegall says, "start by telling her exactly that. Say, 'You know what—I'm not sure how to answer that question.' Then, gently ask her for more specific information. Where did she hear about that, what has she heard, what does she want to know exactly? And then do the best you can. Go to the bookstore together and pull out a book that talks about sex in a straightforward, unabashed way. You can be mortified together, if necessary. She'll be better off if you give her the information she wants and needs. Your daughter is reaching out to you. Reach back, even if you are unsure of yourself."

Cynthia, age thirteen, is from Rapid City, South Dakota, and is uncomfortable telling her mother that some of her friends are getting into drugs. "The situation really makes me tense because I don't want her to hate my friends or worry that I'm hanging out with a bad crowd and going to fail out of school. I don't want it to become a whole big drama."

Girls are more likely than boys to use drugs as a way of dealing with stress or anxiety, according to the Center on Addiction and Substance Abuse of Columbia University. As a result learning how to manage pressure should start at an early age, says Jacqueline Sawyer, a coordinator of Friendly PEER-suasion, a Girls Inc. substance abuse prevention program.

"It's not as if a girl says, 'I'm going to go do something that is destructive to my life,' " she explains. "A girl usually gets into drugs to numb the pain."

Carol Gilligan, a Harvard professor and author of the book *In a Different Voice*, tells how our culture teaches girls to use their voices to "cover rather than convey" the reality of their lives. "Lies make you sick," she writes. "As long as girls continue to be the carriers of unvoiced desires and unrealized potential, they run the risk of losing their voices, their values, and their experiences altogether."

Telling It Like It Is

If you are concerned that a girl you care about feels she has to lie to you about her life, and you would rather know the truth, now is the time to tell her that you support her right to express herself—and that includes her right to tell you things you may find hard to hear: *I'm ready to start dating; My friends are doing drugs; I can't keep up with my schoolwork; I'm pregnant.* One way to do this is through journal writing.

A private journal or diary is not something you and a girl can share, but it is a way for her to process her feelings and beliefs, and to put the truth of her experience into words. A journal can be one place in a girl's life where she says whatever she feels and doesn't have to worry about anyone else seeing or commenting on it. She can be angry, conceited, in love, confused, rebellious, strange, and wonderful.

Writing in a diary is also an expression of a girl's boundaries, since it is so private. You can show your support for her personal discovery and self-expression by respecting that boundary and by helping her to keep her journal safe from exposure.

Another kind of journal is one that the two of you keep together. An interactive journal can function as a private message board where you and a girl can talk to one another about whatever is on your minds. Designate a notebook or set up a private and secure e-mail exchange. Begin by simply keeping each other informed of your daily activities and events. Then, if you both like communicating this way, start introducing topics that are more meaningful, and perhaps more difficult.

An interactive journal can be a place to work out disagreements or engage in an in-depth conversation about a particular topic, a problem a girl is facing, or even a conflict between the two of you. Maybe she will suggest a controversial but not life-threatening topic, such as wanting to get her belly button pierced. The two of you can use the journal to discuss your feelings about the issue without making a decision about it yet. When you do decide on a course of action, you can set terms with one another and keep each other to the bargain.

The journal should be a place where you and a girl can turn off all other stimulus, express yourselves honestly, and deal with one another. Let's say your daughter has heard some sad news recently and is having trouble giving voice to this loss.

She can write about how she feels without being afraid of being questioned or judged. By giving full attention to what is going on in her life and in your relationship with each other, you may start to discover a more direct and compassionate way of communicating outside the journal. You may also avoid a great deal of resentment, confusion, and misunderstanding.

Keep in mind, this is not an occasion for you to treat a girl like a best friend and confidante; it is not a way to invade her private thoughts. Likewise, an interactive journal does not give a girl license to dump all her anger onto you with no follow-up. The tone should be respectful, above all. If a girl reveals something in the journal that you feel the two of you must discuss in person and perhaps deal with more aggressively, say so. But honor the trust that has been established and the boundaries both of you agree upon.

You should let a girl know in advance what you feel you must do or say if you are planning to take her private thoughts, confessions, or disclosures out of the journal and into public space. Keep her involved at all times so she knows she can trust and rely on you.

Speaking Up and Speaking Out

"What if a girl comes up with some great idea that could really make a difference for us girls, but no one ever finds out about it?" asks Anna, a ten-year-old from Atlanta.

A girl figures out early on that ideas can be transformed into actions that will improve her life. She wants to advocate for herself and for her friends, to speak out, and to know that someone is listening to her and cheering her on. In order to do this, a girl needs all the skills and support she can get so she can turn her feelings into a message she can share with others.

"Advocacy helps a girl to develop important communication and negotiation skills," says Brenda Stegall. "Engaging in social change is a great opportunity for women and girls to combine their talents as leaders to make a difference in their community."

Community action is a way to help a girl speak out or organize with others around a particular issue. While community service projects such as collecting clothes for flood victims are indeed admirable and should be very much encouraged, a girl should also become involved with creating longer-term solutions to problems that affect whole communities.

Some examples of the difference between community service and action are:

- *Painting an elderly person's home (community service); setting up a resource network of skilled volunteers or craftspeople willing to donate their time to paint or repair houses in the community (community action).*

- *Collecting money to help a needy family (community service); organizing a food co-op or community garden so that residents can more effectively manage their household needs (community action).*

- *Making a dinner for the local homeless people (community service); working with local groups, including people who are homeless, to address the causes of homelessness (community action).*

- *Donating toys for kids to a battered women's shelter (community service); writing a play about child abuse and performing it at different schools to inform other kids about child abuse and what they can do about it (community action).*

- *Telling kids at school to avoid a dangerous intersection (community service); getting the school to post a crossing guard at a dangerous intersection or getting the city to increase the walk time for a traffic light (community action).*

"Community action motivates a girl to take the next step," explains Ms. Stegall. "Why should a girl's commitment stop at bringing food to people who are homeless every Christmas? She should also become involved in making sure that people don't live in shelters in the first place. A girl can be taught how to research a problem, brainstorm possible solutions, and then come up with a plan for change. For example, a group of girls may decide to invite their mayor to speak at their school or community center to discuss how the city is addressing the problem of homelessness. Or they may want to lobby the City Council to allocate more money for additional low-cost housing or more mental health treatment centers."

Ms. Stegall tells how when two young children were hit by a car on a busy street corner near a Girls Inc. center, the girls in the program advocated posting a crossing guard and installing a traffic light. "They told their ideas to adults who then put them in touch with the decision-makers," says Ms. Stegall. "They used their voices to make a difference."

In *See Jane Win,* Sylvia Rimm discusses childhood influences that have contributed to women's satisfaction, self-fulfillment, and professional success. Of 1,000 women interviewed, about one in three said they were involved in student government in school. In fact, women who had established themselves in careers in government and law were among those most likely to have been involved with student government and/or a debate team in high school.

A girl who does not experience her own leadership is less likely to believe that it is possible to make an impact on her own life, let alone affect the lives of a whole community. The Girls' Rights Survey found that 47 percent of girls say it's true that "people don't think girls are good leaders." And 47 percent don't like it. Girls are ready for the chance to be leaders and to be respected for their ideas and talents at home, at school, and in their communities.

"My eight-year-old daughter and her friends were home once when I was doing some work around the house," says Valerie, a computer programmer from Detroit. "I needed a ladder, so I asked them if they would bring it to me from the garage. They got so into it! Deciding who would carry the front and who would carry the back, telling each other to be careful, guiding it around the corners—it was fun to watch them finding a solution together and taking charge like that."

The following activity will help you guide a girl to see the many ways she is using her voice, her feelings, and her right to speak up as an expression of her leadership abilities. Together, check off the skills that she has accomplished. Keep the list handy so you can add to it over time.

Leadership Skills Checklist
Communications

- I've called someone I did not know.
- I've led an activity in a group, school, or club.
- I've worked in a group to make a decision.
- I've explained my ideas to someone.
- I've used the library to do research.
- I've used a computer to do research or send a message.
- I've interviewed someone.
- I've made a presentation to a group.
- I've listened to others in both small and large groups.
- I've learned new words.
- I've written a letter asking for something (for example, to invite a community leader to a meeting or to request information from a newspaper, library, or other organization).
- I've called on local community leaders to support an issue or program that I cared about.
- I've spoken out in a group my first time there.
- I've introduced myself to someone from a different neighborhood, city, or country.

Relationships

- I've gone out of my way for someone in trouble.
- I've helped someone else meet her goals.
- I've made a decision within my group of friends.
- I've done something a little bit scary but important for me to do.

- I've talked with others in my community about my concerns.
- I've found other people to work with me to make a change.

Planning

- I've developed a plan of action.
- I've completed my group assignment on time.
- I've revised a plan to meet the goal of a group.
- I've revised a plan to meet my own goal.
- I've reflected on those things that are hard for me to do and those that are easy.
- I've kept notes about a meeting I attended.

Creativity

- I've made up a game or activity for a group.
- I've made up a story or song and shared it with the group.
- I've kept a journal.
- I've written a song or poem or made a picture or created some object about girls and women and connected it to my own life.

When a girl gets to the point where she believes she can effect change, even in small ways, she begins to feel more connected to her environment and more invested in improving the quality of her own life. As she begins to understand the impact and power of telling people what she thinks, she is inspired to speak up and make her voice heard.

Ways to Empower a Girl to Express Herself

- *Make sure a girl has one place where she feels free to express herself in the ways that appeal to her talents and sensibilities.*

- *Pay attention to the values and viewpoints a girl expresses. Let her know what interests you about what she is saying and begin a conversation about why she feels a certain way.*

- *Support a girl who is in the process of changing her point of view and help her hold on to views that do not necessarily match the views of her friends or people and institutions in authority.*

- *Teach a girl skills that help her to think on her feet, make her points, and defend her positions without apology.*

- *Discourage a girl from expressing herself in a tentative, questioning, or approval-seeking manner.*

- *Help a girl find ways to express difficult or confusing feelings.*

- *Encourage a girl to find ways to express herself honestly with you and with her friends in the interests of building trust.*

- *Remind a girl that as long as she is not endangering herself or someone else, it is okay to keep personal information about herself and others private.*

- *Share decision-making authority with a girl so her voice has a significant impact on her own life and the lives of others.*

- *Create opportunities for a girl to be a leader. Let her choose the activity, make the rules, settle the disputes.*

- *Encourage a girl to talk as much as she wants and listen intently to what she says.*

- *Suggest that a girl and her friends write, sign, and mail a letter to the mayor, school board, or the editor of the local newspaper about a particular issue they feel is important.*

- *Recommend that a girl start a group where she and her friends can discuss their feelings about a problem, offer possible solutions, and create a plan of action.*

- *Encourage a girl to organize a "speak out" where she and her friends can express their views on a particular topic to their teachers, members of the media, or the leaders of a neighborhood organization.*

- *Suggest that a girl start her own Web site or "zine" (a self-published magazine she fills with her writing, artwork, poetry, and anything else she likes).*

- *Assist a girl in her advocacy efforts by helping her raise funds, get to and from meetings, prepare her letters and publications, or simply by standing by and admiring her energy and enthusiasm.*

3.

Taking Risks and Achieving Goals

"I don't intend to be an average person.
I intend to be very happy."
—JORDAN, AGE NINE

T he sun is hot today, but Amy's legs burn from the inside out with the energy it takes to run up the steepest part of this three-mile course. She and her cross-country team trained all summer in the heat, humidity, and pouring rain to earn the right to compete here at state finals. Up ahead, Amy sees her friend and teammate, Keisha, stride past a girl who's known as the fastest and strongest runner in this race today.

Go, Keisha! Amy thinks to herself proudly, as she wipes the sweat from her forehead and feels an extra burst of adrenaline propelling her forward. Amy has been keeping pace a few steps behind the girl in front of her for the last mile. She hears her coach's words in her head telling her a million times how good she is on these inclines. As soon as I get up to the top, Amy thinks to herself, I'm passing this girl. I know I can do it.

> **Girls'**
> **Bill of Rights**
> **#3**
>
> Girls have the
> right to take risks,
> to strive freely,
> and to take pride
> in success.

A girl thrives when she knows what she wants, takes risks to go after it, and believes in her ability and her right to enjoy all her successes. With the loving, courageous support of the people who matter most to her, she can achieve anything she sets her mind to.

"Girls Inc. focuses on adventure, healthy competition, and all kinds of goal-setting as a way of inspiring a girl to take risks to explore her potential," says Isabel Carter Stewart. "Local chapters plan outdoor adventure and risk-taking activities for girls from the age of six on. This can include rope climbing, sailing, rappelling. We want a girl to experience adrenaline highs. But we also encourage intellectual and emotional adventures—for example, traveling to the city if you're from the country, spending time on a farm if you're an inner-city kid, going to the mountains and to the ocean. It expands a girl's view of the world and her potential."

As you encourage the girl in your life to express strong feelings and ideas, the next step is to make sure she has endless opportunities to channel that energy into the pursuit of her dreams and goals. The Girls' Rights Survey reveals that 50 percent of girls say they experience stereotypes that limit their right to take risks, strive freely, and take pride in their success. Younger girls are more likely than older girls to say they experience stereotypes related to this right. The survey also shows that:

- *47 percent of girls say it's true that people think girls are weird if they plan to be firefighters or police officers.*

- *44 percent of girls say it's true that the smartest girls in school are not popular.*

• *59 percent of girls say it's true that girls are told not to brag about things they do well.*

And the girls don't like it at all. Raising a girl to believe that it is more important for her to be likable than powerful, self-effacing rather than self-promoting, helps to ensure her own defeat. She learns that she can be good at something, but not so good that she will intimidate adults or her peers. She can take risks, but not if those risks challenge traditional ideas about what a girl can handle or accomplish on her own. She can be proud, but she shouldn't let it go to her head because it's not considered attractive. The belief that decisiveness and the ability to say what you want and to go after it are not feminine traits can go a long way in sabotaging a girl's plans for success.

"Living purposefully demands a certain degree of risk, and I don't mean the kinds of risks that are dangerous to a girl's health or her well-being," explains Girls Inc. Director of Research Dr. Heather Johnston Nicholson. "A girl must be empowered to go out on a limb sometimes, to test her abilities, to stretch her muscles, and to feel the thrill of chasing her dream. She also needs support when encountering the obstacles and roadblocks she'll be sure to run into along the way. You can make a huge difference in a girl's life by taking her dreams and goals as seriously as you would take her problems and her difficulties. You will be amazed at the results."

Sherry, a mother of two daughters, from Santa Fe, New Mexico, says, "I didn't get the kind of support I give my kids. For example, my oldest daughter has taken gymnastics since she was five years old. At about age eight, she started finding excuses not to go anymore. I would be in the driveway honking the horn, waiting for her so I could drive her to class on time. She would say she forgot what day it was, or she had a stomachache, or she couldn't find her leotard.

"Instead of yelling at my daughter like my parents would have done to me, I asked her what was up, and she said she wanted to quit. When I asked why, she told me she was afraid of failing, of not being as good as she used to be. We were able to discuss her feelings and calmly decide whether she needed to take a break from gymnastics or simply to get some reassurance at a time when she is developing new skills. I told her that even when you are good at something, taking it to the next level is always hard. And I think she was relieved, because how else would she know that? Being good at something doesn't mean it isn't going to be hard. The question is, is it worth it to you?

"My desire for both my girls is that they will feel confident and be able to go with the flow. I want them to do what they like to do and not be intimidated by others who have different talents. My own mother was not a good role model in teaching me how to do this. In a way, I am spurred on by my own disappointment with what I was not taught. But I have a good friend who's a social worker and when I have a problem with one of my daughters, I turn to her for advice and help."

When you were a girl, did you get the support and encouragement you feel you needed from the adults in your life? Take a moment to consider how you learned about taking risks and going after your goals.

The Road to Success

- *What is the riskiest thing you ever did as a young girl, and what happened as a result?*

- *What is the riskiest thing you ever did as a teenager, and what happened as a result?*

- *What do you consider to be your greatest accomplishment? What was the risk involved in pursuing that goal?*

- *What do you consider to be your biggest mistake? You may have positive or negative associations, or both, regarding this event or decision.*

Chances are that many women, and maybe you, have been dealing with others' low expectations of what you can achieve extending all the way back to your own childhood. This can serve as an additional incentive in your efforts to be there for a girl as she struggles to be "the best" at whatever she does.

Remember to engage with the girl care about as she sets out on the road to her success. One mother realized how often she was telling her daughter to lower her expectations during a workshop facilitated by Girls Inc. The daughter drew a picture of her mother saying the words, "Life is not fair." When the two of them spoke about this later, the mother saw it as a perfect illustration of what she had also learned growing up. Afterward, she said to her daughter, "I do say that a lot, don't I? Maybe too much."

A girl will welcome the benefit of your experiences, including examples of what has worked or not worked for you. Observe how she responds to challenges that lead her in the direction of her goals, and help her to discover the skills and strategies she needs to take advantage of opportunities as they come up.

The following activity will help you find out more about a girl's comfort level and interest in different types of risk-taking adventures.

Rating Risks

Ask a girl to label these examples of healthy risk-taking behavior as *easy, maybe*, or *no way*, based on what she considers a high- or low-risk endeavor. After she has finished giving her answers, tell her how you would rate the following risks for yourself.

- Introduce yourself to someone you haven't met.
- Ask someone where he or she comes from.
- Be a vegetarian when none of your friends are.
- Admit that you don't know how to do something.
- Ask someone for help with your homework.
- Ask an adult for help with a personal problem.
- Hang out with someone your friends don't like.
- Register for an advanced class that none of your friends are going to take.
- Wear your favorite color nail polish (green, black, blue, bright red), even if it's out of style.
- Try out for a sport you've never played before.
- Try out for a sport your friends aren't interested in.
- Raise your hand in class when you think you know the answer.

- Raise your hand in class to ask a question.
- Become friends with someone who's not popular.
- Stand up for someone who is being treated unfairly.

Take this opportunity to suggest specific risks you know a girl is facing, such as confronting a best friend who hurt her feelings, standing up to a bully, or telling a grown-up that she doesn't like something another person does. It may be fun to add other risks that are purely adventure related, such as scuba diving, rock climbing, traveling abroad, or riding the fastest upside-down roller coaster in the universe. If a girl is very young, the risks may be learning to ride a bike, taking ballet lessons, or walking in the ocean up to where the water meets the tops of her knees.

This activity lets you and a girl explore how ready-for-anything or reluctant she is, so you can figure out together what kind of encouragement, opportunities, and guidance might appeal to her at this time. You can also offer yourself as her own private cheering section, her partner and guide. By testing out your own feelings about various risks, you also gain a better grasp of what threatens and inspires you—both as an individual and as a person who is concerned about a girls safety as well as her success.

Go Get 'Em!

"My niece is really adventurous," says Judith, from Omaha, Nebraska, who has an eleven-year-old nephew and a seven-year-old niece. "She loves horseback riding and she's thinking about becoming a jockey or horseback riding teacher. Even though both of them are extremely capable in their own ways, I know my niece will run into more obstacles than my nephew because she is female—I certainly did. I don't want to give her any reasons to doubt herself, so I focus on the similarities between her and her brother, as well as on their individual strengths."

A great deal of what limits both boys and girls are the expectations people have about what boys are "naturally" good at versus what girls are "naturally" good at. Setting boys and girls up to compete with one another for control of these different areas, however, only serves to limit the options of both groups.

A 1999 report by the Horatio Alger Association found that boys and girls are equally likely to list computer programming, math, and science as subjects they consider important. The U.S. Department of Education also reports that girls and boys have similar math and science proficiency scores, and, in general, both groups take advanced science courses because they do well in them or because they are interested in them.

There is, however, a gap between boys' and girls' interests and their perceived ability to do well in these subjects. Sandra, fourteen, from Alexandria, Virginia, tells a story about how she sold herself short in the sixth grade because she felt intimidated by a boy in her science class. "I was in a special math and science class at school," she explains. "In one assignment, we were supposed to team up and make rockets; whichever team made the rocket that went the furthest, won. However, my team knew that one boy who loved to build rockets would most likely win, and we didn't even try to compete. Instead, we decided to make the best-*looking* rocket. We decorated that thing so many times that when it finally came time to fly it, it was so heavy with paint and glue it just fizzled.

"Now when I look back on that, I see how silly it was for us to not even try. If we had asked the teacher for help, we might have actually learned something about rockets. The boy would probably have won anyway—not because he's a *boy*, but because he was really into rockets. Who knows what we could have done—we didn't even stay in the game!"

Mildred Kiefer Wurf, director of public policy of Girls Inc., describes the importance of the 1972 federal education bill Title IX in making it possible for girls to get into both the academic and athletic game—and stay in.

"Title IX changed everything," she explains, "because it called for equal spending among males and females in any educational institution that receives federal funds. With Title IX, more women were able to enter professional schools and to study business, law, architecture, and medicine. In addition, many more women became involved with sports and athletics, and schools across the country began to introduce more teams for girls.

"What a difference! Now, girls' soccer and basketball are broadcast on national television, and to a larger extent than ever before, girls' participation and talent in sports are considered givens. All these accomplished women athletes are out there now, and girls, boys, men, and women know their names *and* their stats. It's a fact of life, and there's no turning back."

In 1971, fewer than 300,000 high school girls participated

in school-sponsored sports. The year after Title IX was passed, that number had nearly tripled to 820,000. In 1998, more than 2.5 million girls played sports in their high schools—almost ten times the number as in 1971.

"Before Title IX, we had no teams, no money, no coaches, and only a handful of role models," continues Ms. Wurf. "Most of us growing up did not have female competitive sports figures to look up to. Today we have soccer star Mia Hamm and basketball star Theresa Weatherspoon. Girls love them!"

Among youth soccer leagues, girls now represent 45 percent of players, according to a 1999 study conducted by the Soccer Industry Council of America. And since 1991, participation in soccer has increased 37 percent among twelve- to seventeen-year-old girls. The Presidents' Council on Physical Fitness and Sports finds that girls who are athletes in high school have higher grades and standardized test scores, are less likely to drop out of high school, and are more likely to attend college.

Unfortunately, not all girls have the chance to participate in sports at equal levels. A girl may find fewer opportunities to get involved in sports due to a number of factors, including her school's lack of funds, her family's economic status, her responsibilities at home, or her cultural and religious upbringing, which may discourage involvement in athletics or extracurricular activities.

"Team sports are so valuable to a girl," explains Pat Loomes. "She has the experience of relying on the other members of her team and contributing to a supportive environment. She gets to be really physical, to play, and to enjoy healthy competition. A girl begins to feel more positive toward other girls, and in turn, feels more positive toward herself.

"There is a spirit of camaraderie among team members who share a common goal. Each one thinks: We're in this together—the wins and the losses. Each girl also realizes she can't do it on her own, and there's no need to. She can count on her teammates and friends to help her achieve her goals."

A girl who takes risks to achieve her goals will meet the challenges and obstacles she encounters along the way with confidence in her own talents and skills. She will also know that she can rely on her friends, her family, her coaches, and her mentors to guide her through the hardest parts.

Have you talked with the girl in your life about her specific academic or athletic goals? What are her short-term goals? For example, she may be preparing to take the advanced placement calculus exam, or she may want to move up from fourth chair trumpet in the school band to first chair. If she is very young, her goal may be to learn three new songs, read a book that's 100 pages long, or roller-blade from one end of her street to the other and back again—without you skating beside her.

Help a girl to focus on one specific goal and use the following activity to map out a plan for achieving it.

Believe It, Achieve It

• *Encourage a girl to identify a realistic and attainable goal. "Become the best in-line skater in the whole world," for example, is unrealistic and unhelpful to a person who is learning.*

• *Brainstorm together about the steps that are required for her to meet her goal. What kind of practice, rehearsal, training, and studying will allow her to improve her skills gradually, over time?*

- *Once she has identified all the steps she wants to take to meet her goal, map out a course of action on a large sheet of paper. Use time intervals to keep things in perspective: "Every week for one month, I will . . ."; "After two months, I will . . ."; and so on.*

- *This goal time line may turn out to be something a girl would want to hang on her wall or on the back of her door. Encourage her to decorate it any way she wants, using colorful markers, crayons, paints, glitter-glue pens, or other craftsy utensils that appeal to her aesthetic and organizational style. If she likes a more streamlined and subtle approach, she may want to write the whole plan on a regular sheet of notebook paper, fold it up, and put it away for a while.*

- *Each time a girl succeeds in taking one of the steps, encourage her to mark her achievement with a big X, a star, or a phrase such as "I am amazing."*

After a girl has completed her plan, your next job will be to make sure this doesn't become a "map of shame" reflecting all of the ways she's not living up to her own standards. For example, if she consistently avoids the steps or starts to resent the whole project, it may be time to reconsider and change course. It may even turn out that it's not the right time for her to go after this particular goal. Again, tune in to her and let her lead—even if her "lead" is to abandon the project entirely. Take this opportunity to find out what changed her mind or what she would rather be doing.

All Work and No Play (Makes One a Miserable Girl!)

"I'm a nerd," says Deanna, fifteen, from Long Island, New York. "Everything I do in school feels like it's not enough. My parents are both doctors. They tell me to study to become a doctor even though I already told them I don't want to be one. They want me to get good grades, so I set my own academic goals through competition—by trying to get higher grades than my friends. My parents are so happy when I bring home all A's. But then they put even more pressure on me! If I get a 96 on a test, it's like, why wasn't it 100? The more pressure they put on me, the worse I do.

"I keep pushing myself to do better in school, but I want to have a life. My friends go out, they go to parties, some of them have even started dating and having boyfriends. I'm not allowed to go out with my friends unless an adult is there. And even then, my parents make me carry a cell phone. At least that's one thing I have in common with my friends—our parents all force us to take cell phones wherever we go so they can keep track of us. We all hate cell phones. One of my friends just turns hers off and says, 'It's broken.' But I don't have the guts to do something like that. Parties and dating—forget about it! Here I am this nerd-girl with straight A's and what do I get for it? I get to stay home and study even harder. Whoopee.

"I want to grow up and be independent, but my parents don't allow it. They think I'll end up with sex, drugs, and booze. They said it's not that they don't trust *me*, it's that they don't trust what's out there. But I'm going to have to deal with what's 'out there' sooner or later. I *am* going to college, and my first choice is Columbia in New York City. How am I going to find my way around Manhattan when my parents won't let me out of my own neighborhood? I'm not staying here for a minute longer than I have to. I feel enslaved."

There is such a thing as too much achievement and the wrong kind of success. A girl who is constantly achieving in order to please someone else and meet someone else's standards is not getting the skills and life experience she needs to be strong, smart, or bold. She may have straight A's in all her classes, but does she know how to dance? She may be a musical genius by the age of ten, but has she ever gone fishing and not caught a single fish all day? What would happen if things did not go exactly as planned for her or if she was not good at something right away? Would she quit? Would she feel like a failure? Would you?

Life is not perfect, and neither is the girl in your life. She needs to know that there is such a thing as doing something imperfectly, sloppily, backward, and wrong—and the world doesn't end. She also needs to know how to deal with unexpected events and changes in plan without calling you.

"Girls Inc. believes in making sure girls have a lot of fun," says Dr. Nicholson. "Learning should include a lot of laughing. We need to help a girl reduce the stress in her life, not add to it. We begin with a respect for who a girl is now and not just who she will become, and we work from a girl's perspective, rather than an adult's point of view about what a girl needs.

"Our Girls' Rights Survey showed that 65 percent of all girls said 'girls are expected to spend a lot of their time on housework and taking care of younger children.' That's too much. We need to give a girl a break, to do her chores for her once in a while so she can play ball, stare into space for an hour, or sleep in on a Saturday. And as far as being the first and best at everything she does—it's not going to happen. Perfection is not an option for any of us. So what if she didn't win the big race! Was there a pizza party afterward? Did she have fun there?"

The right to succeed is as much about helping a girl learn her own limits as it is about inspiring her to push those limits. The best way to strike this delicate balance is by getting to know the girl you care about, by encouraging her to evaluate her goals and reevaluate them, and by making it possible for her to take some time to decide what's next. She deserves to rest on her laurels for a while. Let her tell you what she's dealing with and how she's reacting to the pressures and the rewards that come with success.

Jeannie, an editor from Santa Barbara, California, says, "My mentee joined the debate team at her school because some of her friends were on the team. After three weeks, she confided to me that she was miserable. I figured maybe the debate coach had put her down, or she didn't like being the new girl on the team. But she told me she simply did not enjoy it. There wasn't anything particularly wrong with being on the debate team, it just didn't interest her. So I said the bad words adults are never supposed to say to kids. I told her, 'Go ahead and quit!' She was thrilled. Then we signed up for a pottery class together. Neither of us was very good at it, but we had a blast!"

A girl will go much further in life if she knows that she

will sometimes feel unsure, have doubts, and make mistakes. A girl gains wisdom and pride in knowing that she can forgive herself the occasional goof or wrong turn, learn what she can from it, and keep going. Encourage a girl to speak to you not only about her successes, great report cards, and first-place awards, but also about her anxiety that she may not make a right decision, her jealousy that someone else may be better, or her growing dissatisfaction with what was once an exciting endeavor.

"I'm beginning to acknowledge that there's a difference between being nervous about my twelve-year-old daughter's well-being and safety, and trying to control her," says Michelle, a real estate agent from Minneapolis. "My daughter is at an age where she needs to be who she wants to be, and she's told me she isn't getting enough space. Now, I can't give her all of the space she wants, but I have started talking to her about the kinds of risks she takes that I feel are dangerous, as opposed to the ones that simply make me anxious. When I don't feel I have a clear head, I ask my husband or my sister to help me out, and show me what I might be missing.

"My daughter and I have started doing a new thing where we tell each other stories about a character we make up. This is great to do in the car, and she loves it. It's almost as if we are both one step removed, so we can be interactive and involved. My daughter gives the character advice, says what she would do in her place. And I do the same thing. We let each other know how we feel through this 'imaginary friend.' I get ideas for stories from my childhood and the mistakes I made."

Sometimes the best way to reassure yourself and a girl is to explore worst-case scenarios and other kinds of dilemmas together. What are you afraid will happen? How does this fear compare or contrast with what she hopes will happen? You need to find a way to go both forward and apart together that doesn't leave either of you feeling wary, worried, or helpless.

The following activity will give you an insight into a girl's fears, her decision-making process, and her ability to consider a wide range of options.

Dilemmas

These dilemmas present a character who is at a crossroads in her life. A girl should decide on a course of action to resolve the problem and move through the dilemma. Encourage her to weigh the risks and demonstrate decisiveness, leadership, and the courage to succeed and/or admit problems and mistakes.

DILEMMA #1: STAY IN THE GAME OR QUIT?

Brianna, eight, tried out for her middle school's softball team as a beginner and made it to the team. Now that practices have started, she is having more trouble than she thought she would. She really likes some of the other girls on the team and feels she will be as good as they, if not better, after she gets more experience. But she gets so frustrated and mad at herself for not doing better, sometimes she wants to quit.

What can Brianna do?

DILEMMA #2: BE RESPONSIBLE AND MISS AN OPPORTUNITY?

At age thirteen, Nikki is the oldest of four children. Her brother is twelve, and her two sisters are four and two. Both her parents work away from home during the day, and, to save money, the baby-sitter leaves as soon as Nikki gets home from school. Then Nikki takes over watching the little ones. Today Nikki heard about a free after-school program that takes girls to a college campus three afternoons a week to study advanced science and astronomy. Nikki loves astronomy. She wants to help her parents, and usually enjoys taking care of her sisters (even though they can be wild sometimes), but she doesn't want to miss this opportunity.

What can Nikki do?

DILEMMA #3: AN UN/EXPECTED TURN OF EVENTS

Abby, seventeen, is at a party that was supposed to be fun, but it's boring. None of her friends came when they said they would, and the girl whose house this is has disappeared. It seems pretty clear that there are no adults at home—even though the girl said they were upstairs. Kids are acting stupid, opening the cabinets and drawers to find liquor and messing with stuff that doesn't belong to them. The worst part is, Abby fought with her mom and dad just to be allowed to come to this party. They trusted her, and now it's turning out exactly the way her parents suspected it would. Her parents told her to call if anything went wrong, but Abby is afraid of admitting she made a mistake and possibly getting in trouble. Still, she wants to go home.

What can Abby do?

Make up other dilemmas based on moments in your own life where you had to do the hard thing: hang in there, stand up to your own parents, or admit you made a mistake. Ask a girl to suggest stories based on what her friends are dealing with in their lives. Rent a movie together that deals with a dilemma similar to one you and she may be facing. When the character is faced with an important decision, hit the pause button, and ask her: "What can this character do to get what she or he wants and keep safe from harm [financial ruin, heartache, etc.]?"

Ultimately, a girl will be making the decisions that will guide her own life. As an adult who cares about her, the best thing you can do is help her to develop the confidence and life experience she needs to make sure these decisions are good and to feel she is her own leader. You can also help her find support apart from you, look for allies and mentors throughout her life, and learn both how and when to ask for help.

Proud of Herself

"When I was young, I was always looking for role models," says Nancy Evans, editor-in chief and co-founder of iVillage.com. "I read every biography of a woman that I could find. Now my role models are girls. I think of my daughter's basketball team playing hard, keeping an eye on each other, elbowing the girls on the other side. And I marvel, how great that girls can be aggressive and play to win! They are putting into place the building blocks to become entrepreneurs, to strive to start and head their own businesses. It's really fantastic."

Jan Roberta from Girls Inc. says, "A girl is inspired to be successful by learning practical ways to reach her full potential.

Once she has the awareness and tools she needs to ensure that she is being treated fairly by the people in charge, she's more likely to have an equal shot at success. A girl passionately wants to be accepted and respected by her peers, her parents, the culture. She likes knowing that she did something that other people respond to positively, that others are excited about her gifts, her special way of expressing herself, and her tenacity in trying to do something well.

"There are so many girls who don't yet know about the choices available to them. It's up to us, the adults in a girl's life, to take her by the hand and show her what's out there—at least as far as we know. And then we need to be able to let go of her hand so she can go much further. We should raise a girl with less *over*protection, and instead, prepare her for life's challenges. By showing a girl concrete examples of what she can do to make her dreams a reality, and by actively sticking by her as she practices and refines these skills, we set her up for big success in life."

Jonetta, a mother from Memphis, Tennessee, says she tries to introduce her three daughters to people she likes and respects, and to take them to places she personally enjoys. "They see that I believe in myself from what I do and how I live," she explains. "The dominant messages I want to communicate to my daughters are for them to be financially independent; to get married because they want to, not because they have to; to not settle on being a flight attendant if what they really want is to be the pilot; and to know if they are ever in danger, they should leave immediately. They must believe in their instincts and not be afraid to second-guess or act on them.

"I'm divorced and I talk a lot with my daughters about what it's like to be a single mom. They can see from my example that a woman doesn't necessarily need a man in her life to be happy and successful. I think adults put too much pressure on kids to be perfect. A lot of time, we don't know some of their problems because they can't tell us every single thing. And then we end up inadvertently adding to their stress.

"My mother started working outside the home when I was in junior high, and that was hard for me. Things were very different then. I never spoke to my mother as openly as my girls speak to me. Sometimes it shocks me, but I don't want them to stop. I always got the feeling my mother could not know and did not want to know what I was going through. So I made a lot of decisions on my own, some bad, some good. I want my daughters to take control of their own lives, to be independent and successful. I help them wherever I can, and if I can't, then I have to trust them to figure things out for themselves. Oh, and of course, I worry. But I know they're smart. They show me they can take care of things."

It is an excellent idea to introduce the girl in your life to successful women, and to make her aware of women of all backgrounds and abilities who have achieved great things throughout history. But be sure and remind her that all women were girls once. Let her know that every person, every celebrity athlete and scientific genius, faces problems and decisions along the way. They make mistakes, and sometimes fail. Every one of these women has some things she is incredibly good at doing, and other things that she is not as good at doing.

In *See Jane Win*, Sylvia Rimm describes the factors that contribute to a girl's success mentality. These include: setting high educational standards for her; coaching her to expect success and pressure in her life; helping her to experience herself as intelligent, a good thinker, and a problem solver; and working with her to help her choose the best educational opportunities and options for her.

Every girl deserves to feel proud of her achievements. The following activity is an occasion for you and a girl to identify and celebrate pride in her accomplishments.

Best Book

Create a book where girl can keep track of all the extraordinary things she does; all her large and small successes; all her special, developing talents; and any wise, courageous, or funny things she says and does. Make time to work on it together. This book should be a source of pride and inspiration, as well as a record of how her talents, interests, and abilities are constantly changing and improving over time.

Use this "best book" as an incentive to help a girl brag about some of her choices that did not lead to complete and total success—she should be proud that at least she tried at something she cared about. A girl who has worked hard, played hard, stayed up late studying, and trained year-round deserves to celebrate herself in a big way. If she does something remarkable, be sure to let her know that she wasn't just "lucky" and she didn't just have "a good day." She knew what she was doing and she did it—despite whatever doubts, strong competition, tiredness, and anything else that might have been in her way. In this way, you can help a girl strengthen her inner voice, the one that will tell her for the rest of her life how capable she is, and how willing she is to work hard to accomplish something truly extraordinary.

A girl's own version of success does not have to be perfect, it just has to be what she wants. She doesn't have to get the best grade in the class, but she should apply herself and get the highest grade that she knows she can get, the one that she will feel proudest to have earned. A girl doesn't have to be the highest scorer on her basketball team, but she can thrive on the thrill of the game and the solidarity of teamwork. When she goes after the goal she chooses, the one that excites and motivates her more than all the others, she will not only achieve great success but will also feel deep down that this success belongs to her and she has every right to enjoy it.

Ways to Empower a Girl to Take Risks and Achieve Her Goals

· *Avoid rescuing a girl. Encourage her to make an imperfect product, to get disheveled and sweaty in pursuit of a goal, and to make big interesting mistakes.*

· *Give a girl bragging lessons. For example, take a girl fishing and if she catches a fish, ask her: "That fish was how big? You fought that fish for how long before you finally landed it?"*

· *Encourage a girl to replace the words "I won't" and "I can't" with "I don't know how" and "I'll try."*

- *Pay close attention to a girl when she is working on something that is difficult for her. Help her develop the skills and confidence to ask for help and, if necessary, to redirect her energy toward a goal that will make her happier.*

- *Teach a girl how to take the time to get more information before she makes a decision.*

- *Help a girl gain experience trusting her own judgement and ability to make a decision. If it will not endanger her or someone else, let her make the choice she wants to make, even though you may feel it is the wrong one.*

- *When things don't go as planned, encourage a girl to learn from what happened, let herself off the hook, and move on.*

- *Help a girl learn to tell the difference between safe risks and unsafe risks by sharing your experiences and asking her about hers.*

- *Encourage a girl to ask herself: Could this risk hurt me? Could it hurt other people? If the answer to both is no, this is probably a low risk, and whatever she chooses will be okay, and it may even turn out great!*

- *Guide a girl as she learns to identify short- and long-term rewards that come with taking a specific risk.*

- *Give a girl lots of support for expressing how she feels about a particular goal, so that she will also feel free to tell you when she's having trouble, or wants to change her mind or her method for reaching that goal.*

- *Encourage a girl to ask herself: Is this what I want, or am I just doing this to please other people or to make them mad? Is it worth it?*

- *Let a girl know that making her own decisions and wanting to achieve an important goal is something to be really proud of.*

- *Teach a girl that it is okay to let success go to her head. Redefine pride as an "attractive" feminine trait.*

- *When a girl goofs, tell her she is still wonderful and amazing, and then do something fun together.*

- *When a girl does something you consider amazing, tell her—and then shout it from the rooftops.*

4.

Accepting and Appreciating One's Body

"I am very beautiful."
RACHAEL, AGE SEVEN

K aren still can't believe it. "My eight-year-old daughter came home from her friend's house crying her eyes out," she says. "I couldn't imagine what had happened, but she was sobbing so hard, I could barely understand what she was trying to tell me. Finally, in a soft, hurt voice that broke my heart, she said, 'Mommy, I want to die. I don't know what to do. I'm so fat and ugly.'

> **Girls'**
> **Bill of Rights**
> **#4**
>
> Girls have the right to accept and appreciate their bodies.

"My daughter is athletic, healthy, and perfectly well proportioned," Karen explains. "She's a terrific soccer player and also loves football. I make it my business not to have fashion magazines in the house, I don't make a big deal about food, and I've never been on a diet in my life. Weight is not an issue in our family. Where was this agony about my daughter's body coming from?"

Karen finally coaxed out the story. Her daughter told her she and three classmates were playing at her friend's house when the girl's mother suggested it would be fun to compare how much the girls weighed. The mother then had them stand on a scale one by one, and she called out the numbers. Karen's daughter was eight pounds heavier than anyone else, and the other girls immediately started making fun of her.

"Her friends began teasing her, saying her thighs were fat and everyone could see them during soccer practice," Karen says. "They also told her that her arms were big and hard from throwing a football. My once self-confident daughter was devastated. She said she didn't want to play sports anymore because she was so ashamed that people would be laughing at her body."

Karen adds that when she telephoned the girl's mother to complain, she was dismissed as being overly sensitive. "This woman actually told me that I should take more of an interest in my daughter's weight—that she could stand to lose a couple of pounds!" Karen exclaims.

When Sara Shandler asked for contributions from girls for her book *Ophelia Speaks: Adolescent Girls Write about Their Search for Self*, she received more than 800 essays: the single most written about subject was eating disorders. In addition, most girls, regardless of their economic, geographical, or cultural backgrounds, said they felt great pressure to be thinner than they were, and that their negative images of their bodies affected their feelings of self-worth.

Girls as young as eight years old express concern about their weight, according to a recent study conducted at Stanford University Medical School. More than one half of the girls in the survey, who ranged in age from eight to eleven, said they were dissatisfied with their weight. More than a third wanted a thinner body, and 16 percent had attempted weight loss. The reasons they gave for wanting to lose weight included teasing by peers, pressure from family, feeling uncomfortable or embarrassed, and wanting to feel better or look better. Three-quarters of the study's participants said they heard about dieting from a parent, while more than half had heard about weight loss from television and other media sources.

In addition, the U.S. Department of Health and Human Services reports that two out of three girls in grades nine through twelve are attempting to lose weight; four times as many twelfth-grade girls as boys take nonprescription diet pills on a monthly basis to lose or control weight; and one in five young women has an eating disorder.

"Girls are terrified of being fat, as well they should be," writes Mary Pipher in *Reviving Ophelia*. "Being fat means being left out, scorned, and vilified. In all the years I've been a therapist, I've yet to meet one girl who likes her body. Girls as skinny as chopsticks complain that their thighs are flabby or their stomachs puff out. And not only do girls dislike their bodies, they often loathe their fat. They have been culturally conditioned to hate their bodies, which are, after all, themselves."

The messages that society communicates to a girl about her body are deeply disheartening. From an early age, a girl is bombarded with messages from the media telling her that body dissatisfaction is normal, dieting is essential, and being sexually attractive is primary. Our culture discourages a girl from developing a strong, athletic body, and dismisses a girl who is perceived as too hard, too dark, too round, or too tall, and pressures a girl to compromise her health to conform to unrealistic standards.

"My aunt told my dad she was worried that I had put on some weight and asked him if I was depressed," says Esther, a senior in private high school in Denver. "As if being skinny would mean I'm happy and being fat means I'm sad! So, without telling me where he got the idea, my dad started suggesting that I go on a diet. I was so surprised and upset, I confronted him right away. When he told me what my aunt had said, I was so mad. I said, 'Look at my grades, look how involved I am in my activities, look at my awards for athletic accomplishments—who cares about my weight?' He felt bad and apologized for not standing up to my aunt for me."

Sixty-two percent of girls in the Girls' Rights Survey say they experience stereotypes that limit their right to accept and appreciate their bodies. In addition, 48 percent of girls believe that the most popular girls in school are very thin.

Being thin and sexy are such powerful ideals for a girl that even if she is not concerned about her weight, she may say she is dissatisfied with her body just to feel included by her peers. "Fat talk is a kind of social ritual among friends, a way of establishing solidarity," writes anthropologist Mimi Nichter in her book *Fat Talk: What Girls and Parents Say about Dieting.*

Like Mother, Like Daughter

It's important to keep in mind how your own attitudes on weight loss and dieting affect a girl's regard for her own body.

A girl also incorporates opinions about how she looks—or should look—from her father, her brothers, and other males in her life.

"The family can play a powerful role in countering the development of eating concerns in young children," explains child psychiatrist Dr. Mary Sanders of Stanford University Medical School. "Parents should talk to their children about the normal growth of their bodies and how dieting is inappropriate for most children."

The pressure for women in our society to be thin, to have a perfectly toned body, and look perpetually young is not lost on their daughters. Josh, an editor for an on-line news service based in Washington, D.C., is worried about his fifteen-year-old niece.

"Caitlan called me the other day to tell me that she's having plastic surgery to get her ears pinned back—she's in tenth grade, for God's sake!" he says. "When I asked her why she wanted to this, she said that she had been really worried that her ears stuck out too much, and her mother, who's my sister, agreed with her. They went to a plastic surgeon who said, 'Sure, no problem,' and is charging them a couple of grand for the operation.

"How can responsible adults allow a young girl to have her body altered permanently at such a young age? It's not only the message it sends that's so harmful—if you're self-conscious about your body, just go ahead and change it—but also the inherent risks of undergoing any kind of surgery. Maybe Caitlan's ears would have looked better proportioned as she got older, who knows?

"I told my niece that I loved her just the way she was. I explained that many people consider it attractive to have their ears stick out a little, that different physical characteristics give you a special uniqueness. She wasn't buying. 'I look in the mirror and I see Dumbo,' she said. 'It's the only thing I think about.' "

In a 1998 survey of more than 1,000 women and their teenage daughters conducted by Yankelovich Partners, 39 percent of mothers said they would approve of their daughters' getting nose jobs, while only 12 percent of the daughters said they would consider these procedures for themselves. In addition, 15 percent of mothers said they would allow their daughters to have breast enlargements.

Author Jean Kilbourne observes that the media promote an ideal portrait of beauty that is almost impossible for women and girls to achieve. "Now we even have computer retouching and ways to make images look inhumanly flawless and perfect," she explains. "The research is pretty clear that the girls who are most susceptible to media messages are those who have the least opportunity to do interesting things or be exposed to people with different perspectives. Girls and young women should be encouraged to compare the images they see on television and in teen magazines—where the actresses and models continue to get thinner and thinner—with their own friends and people they admire of all ages. In this way, they can begin to decide for themselves if they want to buy a certain product or listen to a magazine's advice about how to look and behave."

More than three-quarters of the girls in the Girls' Rights

Survey say that girls are under a lot of pressure to dress right. In addition, in the 1996 Girls Inc. poll on television preferences and viewing habits of the country's school children, girls were more likely than boys to wear their clothes and hair like a person they watched on TV. Twice as many girls as boys also said they had dieted or exercised to look like a character on their favorite programs.

Girls today are faced with many distorted images of an "attractive" female body. Clothes, perfume, liquor, cars, and just about everything are promoted using images of "glamorous, sexy, appealing, ideal" women. Is it any wonder that as a girl approaches adolescence, she begins to question the attractiveness of her own body?

Use the following activity to recall your feelings about your body image when you were your the age of a girl you care about, and then compare them to how she feels about her appearance.

The Ideal Woman

Initiate a conversation, using the following questions as a jumping-off point.

- How did you look when you were the age of the girl in your life?
- How did your friends look?
- How did you feel about your looks?
- What did your mother look like?
- What was your image of the "perfect" body for a woman?

- Who personified that image to you?
- Where did you see this image and how did you come to accept it as the "ideal" body image?
- How did you feel you measured up?

Now, ask your daughter or cousin or neighbor how she would describe how she looks.

- What do her friends look like?
- How does she feel about your looks?
- What is her image of the "perfect" body for a woman?
- Who personifies this image to her?
- Where does she see this image and why does she think it's "ideal"?
- How does she feel you measure up to this image?

Empathize with a girl about her concerns as much as possible without criticizing her desire to fit in or look "as beautiful" as all the other girls. If she sees that you have struggled and, perhaps, still do struggle with appreciating your own body—*and yet you take care of yourself and treat your body with respect*—she learns to lean on you for support and validation, rather than succumb to unrealistic expectations.

A girl's self-image is greatly influenced by today's culture, which is permeated with sex, much of it explicit. The fallout from this speeded-up exposure to provocative images and messages is tremendous pressure for a girl to grow up fast, to be thin like Christina Aguilera and sexy like Britney Spears. For example, the age at which girls are beginning to engage in sexual experimentation is becoming younger and younger. In 1997, 38 percent of fifteen-year-old girls had engaged in sexual intercourse, compared to less than 5 percent in the early 1970s, according to the National Center on Addiction and Substance Abuse.

"Preteens in our culture are eight and nine years of age," says Dr. Ava L. Siegler, author of *The Essential Guide to the New Adolescence*. "We shouldn't wait to talk to them about sex, AIDS, and violence until they are twelve."

"My ten-year-old daughter is completely stressed out about all her friends growing up so fast," says Maria, a sales executive for a large pharmaceutical company. "We live in a typical upper-middle-class suburb outside Philadelphia, and the pressures on the kids here are unbelievable. Cliques are just starting to form in my daughter's class and the 'cool' girls are already wearing halter tops and platform shoes. Some of them are even wearing makeup!

"My daughter is uncomfortable with suggestive clothing—she doesn't like to wear what she calls 'belly-show' shirts. She's also starting to feel left out because her friends are beginning to talk about boys and she doesn't want to join in. Sometimes I find myself wondering if anything is wrong with her, and then I have to remind myself—my daughter is only ten years old. She should have a chance just to be a kid, not a little adult."

You may be sensing that a girl is overwhelmed, angry, or feeling vulnerable to pressures that surround her pertaining to her body and to her friends' bodies. She may be picking up the difference between feeling sexual and feeling like she is *being sexualized*, and it may be extremely difficult for her to give voice to these new insights. The following activity is a good way for you to find out how a girl feels about a particular issue and to show her that you are there to help her sort out the parts that don't make sense to her and that overwhelm her.

Values Voting . . . Again

Encourage a girl to choose from the following responses: *agree, undecided, and disagree,* when expressing her opinion about a value-based statement. These statements relate to her feelings regarding her own body and appearance; how she views other people's bodies and appearances; and her overall physical and sexual comfort level. Keep in mind, these statements are not a "true or false" test; they are values she and you may or may not agree with.

Values Statements:

• *Every person is beautiful in some way.*

• *Being beautiful makes life a lot easier.*

• *There is equal pressure on girls and boys (men and women) to be physically attractive in this culture.*

• *Being underweight is healthier than being overweight.*

• *People are overweight because they are lazy.*

• *Most movie stars and models have the perfect body type.*

- *Boys and men don't pay much attention to women's bodies.*

- *Diet pills are a good way to lose weight.*

- *No one has the right to tell you what to do with your body.*

- *Waiting until marriage to have sex makes you a good person.*

- *If you already said you would do something sexual with another person, you should not change your mind or go back on your word.*

- *If someone wants to be with you and touch you so much that they will be upset if you say no, you may as well be generous and let them do it.*

- *Wanting to be touched in a way that feels good is okay with someone you like and trust.*

- *Sometimes sexual feelings, even pleasurable ones, are confusing.*

- *Talking about condoms as a way to prevent pregnancy and sexually transmitted diseases before having sex ruins the mood.*

- *If someone wants to have sex with you, they definitely love and respect you as a person.*

- *People's feelings change a lot about sex and love; they have to constantly decide between what they want and what they don't want.*

- *Smoking is bad for your health, but it makes people look interesting and mysterious.*

Statements of this kind can be very challenging and even threatening to both you and the girl in your life because they're so personal. They can also be confusing. For example, let's say a girl agrees with the concept that no one has the right to tell another person what to do with her body, but she also agrees with the statement that if you say you'll do something sexual with someone, you shouldn't change your mind. You can help her to articulate her true feelings and beliefs and begin to sort out any apparent contradictions she expresses.

By making it safe for a girl to explore these issues with you, you'll become a tremendous resource to her as she clarifies what's important to her and what she values in her life.

My Body, Myself

Pam and her fourteen-year-old-daughter Lisa are sitting side by side on their living room sofa, sharing a bowl of freshly made popcorn. Pam, a single mother in her early forties, is a French professor at a community college in Miami.

"I've gained weight over the years and am very conscious of my body," she explains. "I associate being slim with being fit and healthy, but Lisa tells me to be proud of how I look, even though I'm overweight. She only gets upset when I let myself go, if I don't comb my hair right or my roots begin to show or I dress sloppily.

"I'm delighted that Lisa is so confident about her body. She's full-figured and loves having what she calls a 'womanly shape.' I was a pudgy child and suffered a great deal growing up. She doesn't seem to mind at all that she's not all flesh and bones—just the opposite!"

Lisa, who recently attended her school prom with a group of girlfriends instead of a date—by choice—is the captain of her softball team and a star swimmer. "Hey, there are all shapes out there," she cheerfully reminds her mother. "I'm comfortable with the idea of my body being wider and larger than the media says is good. I'm part African-American and we're built differently than the models in the commercials and the actresses on television.

"The problem is when I go shopping. The really pretty outfits are made for tall, thin girls. The clothes are usually revealing and skin tight—the popular girls always wear them—and you look stupid wearing them if you're not real skinny.

"Some girls I know are self-conscious and shy about their bodies. I tell them not to worry, that your body doesn't define who you are. The important thing is to take care of yourself for your own sake. But I do know a lot of girls with eating disorders. I paid one of my friends to have potato chips because she stopped eating and I was really worried about her."

Pam and Lisa are very close, although Lisa is beginning to exert a growing autonomy and independence from her mother. "It's taken a while to let go," Pam admits. "Lisa's become very self-sufficient over the past two years. I know I can steer her a bit, but I would never tell her 'no' absolutely without talking about it first. She might go ahead and do it anyway, like most young teenagers. I'd rather know what's going on in her life than have her hide things or lie to me.

"How do we resolve problems? She wears me down! Seriously, I tell her what I think and let it go. I hope she'll listen to what I say and respect my opinion, but I trust her to make up her own mind. I have faith that she'll make the right decision and do the right thing."

The tongue ring incident, however, was a true test of faith between mother and daughter. "It was either that or a tattoo," Pam sighs resignedly. "We battled over that one long and hard. Lisa claimed having a tongue ring or a tattoo was her personal way of expressing herself. That it would make her feel pretty. That it would make her feel proud about how she looked. The tattoo bothered me because it's something permanent, and your tastes are different when you're fourteen than when you're twenty or thirty years old. Lisa did her research and showed me newspaper articles saying that the hole in a person's tongue heals perfectly after the ring is removed. So I reluctantly agreed and let Lisa do it.

"The deal was this, however. The piercing had to be done under completely sterile conditions at a reputable place. Lisa wasn't allowed to complain about the pain—even during the two weeks following the piercing when her tongue swelled up and she was forced to speak with a lisp. To her credit, Lisa didn't say a thing about the discomfort—maybe she just couldn't talk!"

"I could so," laughs Lisa. "But I'm glad the lisp went away. And I think the tongue ring looks beautiful. Knowing that my Mom trusts that I care enough about both her and me not to do anything really stupid, makes me feel very secure and confident."

Open communication between daughters and mothers should start at an early age, especially about issues surrounding a girl's body and her sexuality, according to Maureen Bilger, the former executive director of Girls Inc. of Meriden, Connecticut, who has worked with thousands of girls over the past twenty years.

"Respecting your daughter and having her respect you is key," she explains. "Listen closely to what your daughter tells you, and follow her lead. Remember, you have different opinions from one another, and you must learn to appreciate those differences."

Body image and self-appreciation are key aspects of self-worth. Understanding the differences (and similarities) between how you and the girl in your life regard physical attributes and feminine beauty will help establish a foundation for a continuing frank and open exchange between you about this sensitive topic.

"Unfortunately, girls are not irrational to worry about their bodies," writes Mary Pipher in *Reviving Ophelia*. "Looks do matter." So what should you do if your daughter insists that she needs to lose weight? If your niece says she wants to improve her muscle tone and strength? What kind of physical challenge should you recommend—*other than dieting?*

Physical Challenge

Poor eating habits and lack of exercise can lead to obesity, which is as damaging to a girl's health as starving to be thin. A physical challenge worthy of a girl's time and energy will make her feel healthy, strong, and proud of her accomplishments.

• *Discuss a sport or physical activity that the girl you care for would like to try, or that the two of you could try together. You could take up hiking, join the same gym, take tennis or ice skating lessons together. Set realistic and attainable goals from the outset to help her make measurable and visible changes regarding her physical appearance.*

- *Guide a girl in choosing a new and exciting endeavor—one that involves working with her body's strength and abilities to develop new skills, increase flexibility, and build muscle tone.*

- *Suggest that a girl organize an adventure team with her girlfriends to try different physical activities every month. They should choose something where they can sweat and feel powerful while testing their bodies' abilities and endurance. With your help and by researching different adventure and fitness options on the Internet or in your community yellow pages, she and her friends can become well versed in a variety of different activities.*

A girl who experiences other kinds of physical beauty and strength, apart from models whose collarbones stick out and actresses whose faces look starved and empty, will begin to accept and enjoy her own body, whatever its shape and size.

What's Love Got to Do with It?

Even though a girl learns about the "facts of life" from many sources, parents—particularly mothers—truly are and can be the primary sexuality educators of their daughters. The girl you care for is sorting through myths, mixed messages, double standards, and concerns about getting pregnant and contracting HIV/AIDS and STDs. She may be afraid that her sexuality does not exactly match up with the desires her friends are talking about. Or she may think she knows what she is doing, but she is only basing this on hearsay, on what she's picked up from this friend or that song or a conversation she once overheard.

As adults, we are profoundly influenced by the sexual messages we received when we were young. Those messages affect our attitudes and values today, and determine whether we are comfortable discussing sexual issues with children.

Keep in mind:

- You should try to talk as openly as possible with a girl about sexual issues, even if you're not completely comfortable doing so.
- Be very clear when communicating about sexuality.
- Use your values to guide your behavior.
- Take time to learn more about each other.
- Don't forget your sense of humor!

"A girl should never take risks that jeopardize her future, her life, or her health," stresses Bernice Humphrey, director of the Healthy Girls Initiative of Girls Inc. "It's very important for her to know that even though it's normal for her to have sexual feelings, these feeling should not always be acted on."

Connie, a hospital administrator from Seattle, is the mother of thirteen-year-old twin girls. "All they talk about now is boys," she says. "I hear them giggling in their room, see them staring at their bodies in the mirror, watch them spend hours picking the right outfits, and doing their hair just so. Their hormones are popping, that's for sure! And I want to make myself available to them during this incredibly wonderful but incredibly stressful time in their lives.

"When I was growing up, sex was never mentioned in our house. It was as if it didn't exist. Everything I knew came from my girlfriends or magazines and television. Looking back, I can see that most of what I learned was either incorrect or exaggerated. I figure that since my daughters are going to learn about sex from somewhere, it might as well be from me."

Connie points out that in her day, a girl's biggest fear was getting pregnant. "I wish it were that simple now," she says. "I'm very frightened about the high rate of HIV infection among teenagers, not to mention chlamydia and other sexually transmitted diseases. So last month I sat down with the twins and asked them how they planned to protect themselves when they start to become sexually active.

" 'Mom,' they protested, dragging the word out over several syllables. 'We're not doing anything, don't worry.' I told them I just wanted them to be prepared. That their health and safety and well-being were my paramount concerns.

" 'Okay,' they answered reluctantly. 'I guess we'll use a condom, *when the time comes.*' "

Connie then asked her daughters if they actually knew how to use a condom. After their uncontrollable laughter died down, they confessed they had no idea. Connie told them to go to the kitchen to wait for her, that she would get a condom from her bedroom to show them.

" 'The kitchen?' the twins squealed in unison," Connie continues. "But I knew they were intrigued. Once there, I took a cucumber out of the refrigerator, removed the condom from the packet, and then proceeded to roll it down over the cucumber. There was no laughter now, not even a smile. The

girls were watching me intently, not wanting to miss a thing.
There was nothing dirty or ugly or bad going on. We were
women talking together. I don't want them to learn this—or
learn it wrong!—from someone else."

According to the 1996 Kaiser Family Foundation Survey on
Sex and Teens, one in three girls wants more information about
where to get and how to use different kinds of birth control
methods; more than one in four girls want more information on
how girls get pregnant; and half want more information on how
to prevent AIDS and sexually transmitted diseases. In addition,
two-thirds of girls believe that adults tell teenagers things "when
it's too late," and three-quarters of girls report that adults who
give teenagers information about sex treat them as if they are
unable to make their own decisions.

A girl learns about sexuality every day of her life. She
learns from her friends, movies, videos, television, magazines,
music, and, above all, from the adults in her life. You should be
the one to communicate your values about sexuality and sexual behavior to the girl you care about: it's your right as well as
your responsibility.

Let's say there are some items concerning her health,
appearance, eating patterns, and sexuality that you would like
to talk about, but you aren't sure how to begin. The following
activity will help you to approach a girl safely and gently about
a particular topic.

Conversation Door Openers

Choose from among these "door openers" and complete the
statement with whatever subject you wish to discuss.

- *When I was your age I used to feel* _____.

- *I've noticed that you really like that song. What does it say to you when you listen to it?*

- *I've noticed that you really like that [actress, singer, model]. How does she inspire you?*

- *What have you learned/heard about [menstruation, orgasms, wet dreams, sexual intercourse, oral sex, HIV/AIDS, contraception, homosexuality/bisexuality, masturbation, rape]?*

- *One of the questions I always wanted to ask my parents when I was your age was* _____.
  What have you been wanting to ask me?

- *What would you do if* _____?
  (This is a good opening for a discussion of sexual pressure or abuse.)

- *I've just learned that* _____
  [is pregnant, is struggling with anorexia or bulimia, is severely anemic, was suspended for drug use, dropped out of school, came out to her parents], and I was wondering. . . .

- *I remember I had a boyfriend/girlfriend when I was your age, and I was often unsure of what to do or say. Do you ever worry about that?*

- *There was an article in the paper today about something that happened [at your school, in our community, to a girl your age], and I want to talk with you about it.*

• *I was thinking about what happened in that [TV show, movie, video]. How did you feel about that?*

• *There's a lot of controversy lately about* _____.
How do you feel about that subject?

"You should be straightforward with your daughter, and not wait until a crisis arises to initiate a conversation," advises Susan Houchin, Girls Inc.'s director of national services. "But in order to be effective, you must first be comfortable with what you're discussing—kids know when you feel awkward or embarrassed about something. If you find it too difficult to speak to your daughter about a specific topic, find other people or places where she can have her questions answered. You should also let your daughter know that it's in no way disloyal for her to seek help from other trusted adults if she feels she can't come to you, for whatever the reason."

Having Your Baby

Every year, one in ten young women in the United States from the ages of fifteen through nineteen—or approximately 900,000—becomes pregnant. A girl can choose *not* to become pregnant by understanding she has both the right to say no and the right to determine who, if anyone, is able to touch her body.

How did you learn about sex and reproduction? Did your family use cute or made-up words to describe female and male genitalia, menstruation, and sexual intercourse? If so, what were they? You don't have to be an expert or completely at ease with the topic of sexuality and pregnancy to do a good job of educating a girl about these topics. Although it's best to start talking to a girl when she is very young, it's never too late to start.

Think About

What would you say to your daughter in the following situations?

- *Your nine-year-old starts her period earlier than all of her friends and is upset.*

- *You walk into your fourteen-year-old's room and find her with friends, looking at magazines that contain pictures of naked men and women engaging in various sexual acts.*

- *Your eleven-year-old is good friends with a girl who is thirteen. Today, you find out from a neighbor that the girl is having sex with her much older "boyfriend."*

- *Your thirteen-year-old cannot stop crying because the kids at school have been calling her "queer" and a lesbian.*

- *Your fifteen-year-old asks you for birth control.*

- *Your twelve-year-old wants to start going out on dates.*

- *Your ten-year-old tells you that she really likes a boy in her class. She goes on to say that she got his telephone number this afternoon and plans to call him tonight.*

There are no "right" or easy answers for dealing with any of these scenarios. But your own personal values and your love for a girl will help you decide how to address these situations directly, with honesty and compassion for her well-being. Remember, you don't need to wait for your daughter to ask questions. You can—and should—begin conversations about sexuality, even if you find them somewhat difficult.

It takes practice to develop opinions, both for women and girls. The following role-playing activity empowers a girl to resist unwanted sexual pressure by giving her the actual tools to express her true feelings and desires.

Snappy Comebacks

A girl can learn actual language to respond to comments that try to push her into becoming sexually active against her will. Practice these comeback lines with her until she becomes familiar with them.

Pressure line: If you loved me, you would let me kiss you.

Comeback: I need to talk about this.

Pressure line: You promised.

Comeback: I'm not having this conversation again.

Pressure line: But I love you.

Comeback: You can show me you love me by backing off.

Pressure line: Can I touch your breast?

Comeback: I told you how far I want to go.

Pressure line: If you get pregnant, I'll marry you.

> *Comeback:* I'm not ready to get married or to get pregnant.
>
> *Pressure line:* Come on. Have a beer [drink, drag, sniff, etc.]. It will get you in the mood.
>
> *Comeback:* My mood is fine, and I'm not interested in getting high.
>
> *Pressure line:* You know you want it.
>
> *Comeback:* This is my decision. I'm going home now.

These lines might make a girl laugh, but they're catchy and may pop into her head at the exact right moment. It's good practice for being clear and direct in a situation where the emotional and physical sensations can become confusing. The right to say no is not about feelings: it's about boundaries and communication.

A girl who respects her body respects herself. A girl should be encouraged to be proud of the body she was born with and know that it is both good and beautiful. By accepting and valuing who she is, a girl will be able to make healthy and informed choices about her future.

Ways to Empower a Girl to Appreciate and Accept Her Unique Body

- *Help a girl develop a healthy body image by teaching and showing her that beauty comes in different sizes, shapes, colors, and abilities.*

- *Encourage a girl to develop a personal style that feels comfortable and attractive to her.*

- *Give a girl accurate information about her body so that she can take full charge of her health and hygiene.*

- *Teach a girl the importance of maintaining an active lifestyle and staying drug and alcohol free so that she can build a strong and healthy body.*

- *Discourage a girl from dieting as a means of losing weight or making changes in her appearance. Instead, encourage good nutrition, plenty of fun physical activities, and a new style of clothing or haircut.*

- *Observe your own relationship to weight and appearance. If you notice that a girl has picked up your own tendencies to be critical of your appearance, acknowledge this openly with her. Create a new common ground where the two of you can help each other appreciate how you look and feel.*

- *Discuss stress with a girl while also sharing your experiences of dealing with stressful situations and feelings. Encourage her to explore healthy ways of managing her stress.*

- *Teach a girl to critique beauty ideals for girls and women as they are portrayed in television programs, popular songs, movies, books, and magazines.*

- *Lobby the fashion industry to expand its definition of beauty by featuring more diverse-looking models.*

- *Help a girl explore what she wants from romantic relationships and what she's looking for in a partner. Find a way to offer your insights about healthy relationships without judging her desires.*

- *Teach a girl how to communicate clearly with a date or romantic partner about everything from which movie they will see that night to how far she wants to go physically and emotionally in the relationship.*

- *Work with a girl to come up with lines and phrases to help her deal with sexual pressures, and practice these responses with her out loud.*

- *Counteract the pressure on a girl to feel shame about her body, her sexuality, and her desire to love and be loved. Let a girl know that feelings of pleasure, love, loss, desire, and confusion are a part of everyone's life.*

- *Advocate for health and sex education classes that offer accurate information and place equal emphasis on sexual responsibility for both girls and boys.*

- *Support teenage pregnancy prevention initiatives in your community.*

5.

Being Confident and Safe

M y little sister has always been very sure of herself," says Lee, a seventeen-year-old from Wheeling, West Virginia, and the oldest of four, two girls and two boys. "Since Dara was really young, she always spoke up and said what was on her mind.

"This is Dara's first year in high school. I'm a senior there and really excited about graduating because I got a full scholarship to Duke. Dara found her own group of friends right away, and I was so impressed at how well she adapted. She liked her classes, especially American history. Everyone complains about it being too hard, but Dara was setting the curve on every test.

"By Thanksgiving, she was acting weird. I'd pass her in

> **Girls'
> Bill of Rights
> #5**
>
> Girls have the
>
> right to have
>
> confidence in
>
> themselves and
>
> to be safe in
>
> the world.

the hallway at school and it was like she couldn't see me. She was in a daze. I'd say her name and she'd jump, like I had snuck up on her or something. She was suddenly very spacy and jittery—even at home.

"So one morning on the way to school, I said, 'Okay—WHAT is going on?' Her face turned red and I was like, 'Dara—something is up. You need to tell me.'

"Turns out the teacher from her history class had been *hinting* to her that she felt more like a 'friend' to him than a student, and that she was much brighter and more grown-up than the other girls in the class. He said she had some kind of spark that reminded him of when he was younger. He encouraged her to 'visit' him between classes because he missed her. Then during these visits he started telling her stuff about his life, how he wasn't happy in his marriage, and how his wife never listened to him and wasn't attracted to him.

"Dara said there were these long pauses when they were alone, and he just stared at her until she got the creeps or until the bell rang and she had to leave.

"She told me that maybe she was imagining things or overreacting. She didn't want to say anything bad about him because he's so unhappy and insecure. And I'm like, 'Dara—he's doing a total power trip on you! He's harassing you! He's hitting on you! We have to tell Mom and Dad.'

"So we turned around and went home. On the way, I could see her starting to relax. I think she had been waiting for me to figure out what was going on. Mom and Dad had not left for work yet and were still getting our brothers ready for school.

"Dara told them herself and they were very sympathetic.

I don't know why but I started crying. Then Dara was crying. I felt like I should have been taking better care of her so this wouldn't happen. Mom and Dad got on the phone and demanded to meet with the principal THAT DAY, then brought Dara and me to the meeting.

"The teacher is temporarily suspended, so I don't know what will happen next. Dara handled it really well. And my parents were sort of amazing." Lee smiles and adds, "Now I can go away to college knowing my little sister is safe."

A girl who has confidence in herself is better prepared to handle difficult and potentially dangerous situations calmly and directly. By learning to recognize, trust, and follow her instincts, a girl can take steps to ensure her own mental and physical well-being.

"We must teach a girl the skills she needs to take responsibility for her health and safety without blaming her for being vulnerable to the kinds of danger she cannot control," says Bernice Humphrey, director of the Girls Inc. Healthy Girls Initiative. "Too often a girl learns about danger by hearing from her parents, her school, her friends, or the media that she is likely to be a victim at some point and it is her job to avoid this fate. But all this does is scare her. There's a whole area of a girl's life where she can exercise a great deal of confidence and control to protect herself. She can't control how those around her behave, but she can sharpen her instincts, trust what she sees and what she knows, and use that knowledge to stay as safe as *possible*. That's all we can do for a girl. For that matter, it's all we can do for one another, aside from acting responsibly ourselves."

Traditional feminine upbringing tells a girl that it is of primary importance that she be polite, kind, generous, and a good person. Unfortunately, a girl is also often led to believe that if someone hurts her or if something bad or scary happens to her, she should have "seen it coming" or should not have "brought it on." A girl may even get the message that if someone is especially nice to her, she owes them her care and affection in return. These messages work together to confuse a girl and distort her perceptions, leaving her in an awkward and unsafe position.

"If a girl feels it's her job to please and offer comfort to any person who needs it, she may face what feels like an impossible conflict when others are acting inappropriately toward her," says Bernice Humphrey. "The question becomes: should she be nice and assume this person doesn't mean to hurt her, ignoring what feels uncomfortable to her? Or should she call it as she sees it and get out of the situation without worrying about why this person may be acting a certain way? In order to deal effectively, a girl needs to know how to call things as she sees them. She needs to respond to those gut feelings that tell her someone or something is threatening her safety and security."

There are times when being polite is not effective in getting a strong message across, and when she will need to know and then state her wishes clearly. She needs to understand that sometimes even people she cares about may do and say things that don't feel right or good to her, and that she can set limits and tell people what she wants from them. It is also crucial that the adults in a girl's life reinforce the fact that beyond acting in a safe, aware, and responsible manner, a girl is ultimately not responsible and not to blame for what other people do. It is not her fault if she is hurt, tricked, or betrayed, but there are skills she can develop to try to avoid these painful experiences in the future.

The Girls' Rights Survey reveals that 54 percent of girls and 26 percent of women say that girls experience stereotypes that limit their right to have confidence in themselves and to be safe in the world. A significant number of girls also say that people think it's not important to teach girls how to protect themselves, and they don't like it.

"Utopia for girls would be a place in which they are safe and free, able to grow and develop in an atmosphere of tolerance and diversity, and protected by adults who have their best interest at heart," writes Mary Pipher in *Reviving Ophelia*. The best way to bring about a safer world for all girls is by inviting every girl to take an active role in caring for and protecting her own best interests and by offering to be her partner and guide in that process.

Early Memories

As you teach a girl how to keep herself safe and healthy, it may be helpful to first consider how safe or unsafe you felt as a girl—in your home, in your school, and in your community. Take a moment to answer the following questions:

• *Under what conditions did you feel the most safe at home, at school, and in your community when you were growing up? Why? For example: You may have felt safe at home only when both of your parents were there, or only in certain areas of your school. Complete the following sentences:*

"I felt safe at home when . . ."

"I felt safe at school when . . ."

"I felt safe in my community or neighborhood when . . ."

• *Can you remember what you were afraid of when you were the age of a girl you care about?*

• *Would you describe yourself as having been confident in your feelings and in your ability to handle scary situations as a girl? Why or why not?*

If you were raised to ignore rather than deal with conflict, you may feel intimidated by the challenge of teaching a girl to trust and stand up for herself. If you were taught that danger and accidents happen only to people who are weak or who invite their suffering by being foolish, you may struggle with feelings of shame about negative or frightening experiences you had growing up. You may even have been subjected to verbal, physical, or sexual abuse in your home.

Perhaps the people who raised you felt so helpless in the face of all the ways you might get hurt, they simply told you: "Don't get hurt," without offering you any skills or awareness about how to do this. Maybe they themselves were traumatized growing up and inadvertently taught you that danger lurks everywhere, is unavoidable, and there is much to fear.

If worrying about the safety of the girl in your life keeps you up at night and causes you to feel that the only way to protect her is to *over*protect her, take heart. Learning to trust a girl to make strong, smart, and bold decisions about her health and safety requires tremendous courage. Recognizing that it is not up to "fate" to keep her safe from harm is the first step toward protecting you both.

By teaching a girl how to keep herself safe, how to stand up for herself, how to address conflict, and how to avoid people and situations she considers threatening, she will develop courage and self-confidence. And you will go to sleep knowing that she possesses the self-defense skills and awareness she needs to make her world a safer place.

Creating and Protecting Private Space

A girl is already making choices about what she wants to have happen and what she wants to avoid all the time. She wants to play outside; she wants to read in her room with the door closed; she wants to get the lead in the school play. If any of these activities were expected of her or forced on her, she would be likely to enjoy them less or not at all.

It is important to focus on chosen and wanted experiences as you teach a girl how to assert directly her desires and how to say no to experiences she does not want. There is a correlation between the decision-making process over mundane, everyday activities and bigger issues, such as feeling comfortable in sexual situations. The more responsibility a girl has in her own life, the safer and more empowered she will be to assert control in potentially harmful situations.

This next exercise has many parts, and you may prefer to do them one at a time instead of all at once. Each part will give you and a girl the tools you need to explore and define safe space and to create boundaries that are flexible yet firm enough to withstand real-life situations.

A Girl's Castle

Consider the way a castle is built. It is large with many rooms, upstairs and down. A castle holds and keeps safe the treasures of the person who lives there. It may have towers with windows and lookout posts at the top that let the person see a great distance out to what's on the horizon and what is coming closer. Immediately surrounding the castle, there may be a wide moat filled with water. In order for anyone to enter the castle, a bridge must be lowered to carry the guest safely over the moat and past the gates. To be invited into someone's castle is a privilege and an honor. Once there, it is naturally expected that the guest will treat the person who owns the castle and its treasures with care and respect. The honored guest, too, can expect to be treated with care and respect while in the castle.

A girl's castle is designed to keep her and all her treasures safe, cared for, and respected. Her treasures are not people, animals, or things, but rather her most private self: her thoughts and ideas, her heart's desires, her body and all her senses, her muscles and her unique strengths, the love she feels for herself and for others, her feelings, her judgments, her needs, and her wants.

The moat surrounding the castle is there for a reason—not to keep her in and everything else out, but so that a girl can always *choose* what she invites in as well as what she lets out. The "gates" and "bridge" function as a means for letting her own ideas, feelings, and demands come out, and also as a means for bringing new ideas, feelings, and outside demands—or "guests"—in.

A castle without a moat for protection is vulnerable to invasion. In the same way, a girl without boundaries is vulnerable to being invaded and overwhelmed by other people's opinions, demands, and desires. With no moat, no bridge, and no gate to create a barrier, "guests" can come waltzing in as though they belong there. If she has no boundaries, a girl may see these things in her space and feel obliged to care for them and treat them as she would her own treasures—only they are not her treasures. They are guests, and she did not invite them.

- *Encourage a girl to draw a castle on a sheet of paper and a circle around the castle. (Drawing two concentric circles works just as well.)*

- *Inside the "castle," have her write words that describe her "treasures." These are the things that make up her most private and unique self. Focus on:*

  1. *the activities she enjoys most of all*

  2. *the feelings in her body that are pleasurable (feeling good and full after a delicious meal, feeling that she just said something smart and funny, feeling warm, feeling cool, etc.)*

  3. *the feelings she has for herself (love, respect, understanding, etc.)*

  4. *the feelings she has for others*

  5. *the things she needs and wants (food she likes, a comfortable place to sleep, to be safe, loved, and protected, etc.)*

• *Outside the circle that surrounds and protects the "castle," have her write about possible "guests." These are the experiences, feelings, and ideas she may choose to invite into her space. For example:*

1. *having an adventure or going to a place she has always wanted to go*

2. *a hug or a kiss from someone she loves*

3. *being held by someone who holds her just the way she likes*

4. *holding hands with someone she loves*

5. *having her hair brushed or braided or stroked by someone who does it just right*

6. *being told that she is special, strong, beautiful, talented, and other great-feeling adjectives*

7. *being taught a new skill or a new way of doing something, such as riding a bike, opening her eyes underwater, or thinking about a person she already knows in a new and different way*

Affection and physical play—even from you and other people she loves—belong outside the moat. This tells a girl that she is in charge of her own pleasure and comfort, that she can choose to be held, choose to show affection, choose the kind of play, and choose to be left alone by anyone at anytime.

You will sleep better at night knowing that the girl in your life can tell the difference between choice and coercion, between an open invitation and manipulation or persuasion. In the face of a tricky character or situation, she will have the ability to know at once: This person does not respect me. This is not who I want in my castle.

Not in My Castle

Now take out another sheet of paper and have a girl label this one: Not in My Castle. On this paper, encourage her to write all of the feelings, experiences, and ideas she does not want or appreciate. For example:

1. being yelled at

2. being hit, punched, pinched, knocked over, or hurt

3. being told she's stupid, ugly, clumsy, a brat, selfish, not going to make it in life, not good at something she enjoys doing, etc.

4. feeling scared, all alone, like a prisoner, like a bad person, like everything she says and does is wrong

5. being tickled too hard or past when it feels good

6. being held, kissed, tickled, swung around, or even talked to by someone she doesn't like

7. being teased, tricked, or lied to

8. finding out that someone told her secret or went to a secret place of hers

9. keeping a secret that makes her stomach hurt or get butter-flies inside

This list may go on and on, just as a girl's chosen and wanted experiences—or "guest" list—may also go on and on. The most important thing to emphasize through this activity is the fact that a girl can exercise a clear choice. She can literally draw a line between what she wants and can choose to have happen, and what she definitely does not want. In this way, you are intro-ducing her to and reinforcing her power. She has the power and the right to make herself feel good, as well as the power and the right to avoid feelings, experiences, people, and situations that do not feel good to her.

The final portion of this activity involves giving a girl the language she will need to assert her power.

Telling It Like It Is

Many adults do not understand that even if their intentions are to delight a child and to show love, a child is never obliged to kiss or be kissed, to be tickled, to be picked up and held, to be hugged or petted, or to be good-natured when she feels some-one is making fun of her. A girl needs to know that:

• *It is not acceptable for someone to get into her space without first ask-ing her for and then getting her permission.*

• *It is acceptable for her to say TO ANYONE AT ANY TIME: "Stop" and "Wait." If someone is being aggressive, rude, or frightening her, she will need to be assertive and, possibly, aggressive in protecting her boundaries.*

If a girl has concerns about hurting someone else's feelings or being impolite, explain that when someone is doing something she doesn't enjoy, it is always best to say so directly. When the person respects her wishes, it is fine to say thank you. Take this as an opportunity to discuss the ways that respecting another person's boundaries and asking them to respect yours builds trust and shows the other person that you want to have a good relationship with them.

Revisit the list she created to show what was NOT welcome in her castle. How would she respond if these (not dangerous) experiences came knocking at her door? Use the clear, direct language below to help her practice voicing her desire to keep unwanted attention, experiences, people, and demands out of her space.

The Language of Boundaries

I don't want to be hugged right now.

I don't like that.

I don't want you to do that.

I don't want to do that.

That hurts.

You're making me dizzy.

That's not funny.

You're hurting my feelings.

Please stop that.

I told you no.

Get away from me.

If you witness or observe that an adult friend or relative is acting inappropriately toward a girl you care for, let that person know what bothers you and why. Make sure she does not have to deal with this behavior in the future. If she wants to know why that person is never around anymore, tell her the truth: "That person was doing something I didn't like, and refused to stop doing it. So I told them to stay away."

If a girl is being hurt or is in real danger, obviously, the statements above are not appropriate. In those instances, she will need to get away from the situation and/or get help immediately. Other activities in this chapter will help you teach her how to handle more threatening situations calmly and effectively.

Resolving Conflict

"My friend Erin, from my junior varsity volleyball team, and I used to be really close," says Toby, fourteen, from Amarillo, Texas. "But she started smoking pot with her older sister and her sister's friends. She always invited me to come with them when they were hanging out. I told her I wasn't into it, and she was fine about respecting my decision. But she spends more time with them than she does with me, and we are growing apart. It's awful, because I don't want to smoke pot, but I also don't want to lose my friend."

It takes practice to develop boundaries and opinions that can stand up under pressure. "A girl needs to identify what the pressures in her life are in order to think about how she might respond when challenged," says Jan Stanton. "Setting limits can be really hard, and the answers are not always so black and white. Just because someone is pressuring a girl to do something she *knows* she doesn't want to do, doesn't mean she has the skills to say so without feeling awkward or unsure.

"We walk a girl through the whole interaction—from the moment she is faced with a conflict to the point of speaking her opinion and all the way through to the dealing with people's responses to what she has said or done. Then, we go beyond that to explore how she feels about what just occurred. Being brave is not easy. If it was, we'd all be brave all the time."

It's important to make room for the emotional cost of speaking up and speaking out in the course of teaching a girl the difference between what is right and what is wrong, and between what is good for her and what is bad. "A girl who is trying to be brave about how she lives her life needs the adults in her life to acknowledge how painful it is when those decisions cause her to lose the people she once cared about," explains Ms. Stanton. "It is a loss when her friends become heavy drinkers and she can't hang out with them anymore. It is a loss when her boyfriend calls her a prude for not sleeping with him and then starts dating someone who will. It doesn't matter that he's a jerk—he's a jerk who she liked."

While girls report that drugs become easier to get in high school, they also note that, as they get older, parents and teachers are less likely to talk to them about the harmful effects of drugs. One in three girls in junior high school and four out of ten girls in high school report that their parents seldom or never talk to them about problems associated with alcohol and other drugs. And a 1999 study of an Ohio teen line showed that alcohol and other drugs are the number one concern of teens. One in ten calls regarded a personal problem with drugs or alcohol, and seven out of ten teens said this was the biggest concern facing teens.

Discussing sexual topics is also particularly sensitive. A 1999 report by the Henry J. Kaiser Foundation showed that over one-third of fifteen- to seventeen-year old girls say that they would be uncomfortable discussing STDs with their sexual partners. Over two-thirds agree that "it is often more embarrassing for couples to talk about sexual issues, like STDs, than to have sex."

Supporting a girl also means supporting her reality. "All girls need help making sense of the sexual chaos that surrounds them," writes Mary Pipher. "They need help separating affection from sex."

Even if she has the practical skills she needs to make her environment as safe as possible, a girl still faces the emotional challenge of dealing with the discomfort and consequences that come with standing up for her beliefs and her health. She needs to know how to address and resolve conflict and its aftermath in relationships with people she loves and people in authority, and to handle disagreements and difficulties with her friends, her romantic partners, her teachers, her employers, and you.

Jaelynn, a restaurant owner from Philadelphia, says, "I try not to carry my anger over after my daughter Angela and I have a disagreement. I want her to experience fighting fair and know that our relationship will survive us being mad about a particular issue. Instead of saying, 'I'm mad at you,' I say, 'I'm mad about this.' And likewise, I don't want to hear her shouting at me, 'I hate you, Mom!' I want to hear, 'I think you're wrong,' or 'I totally disagree.' I can work with that."

The next activity, adapted from Girls Inc. Will Power/ Won't Power program, will help you engage a girl in conflict resolution while you both stay one step removed from the action and the emotional risk.

Dilemmas—Passive, Aggressive, and Assertive Behavior

- *Together, look up the words* passive, aggressive, *and* assertive *in the dictionary. Read these definitions out loud to one another.*

- *Once a girl understands these terms, consider the following dilemmas. She should be able to determine whether the characters are acting passively, aggressively, or assertively in a conflict. Help her to figure out how she would handle the situation by asking her the questions posed after each dilemma.*

DILEMMA #1: ORDERING FOOD IN A RESTAURANT

Deanna and her friends are out to eat at their favorite restaurant. She ordered a hamburger well done. When the waiter brings her burger, she takes a bite and it's pink inside. Deanna shouts "Ugh! This is sooo disgusting!" and starts making loud vomit noises. She then calls the waiter over and says, "This burger is RAW! You better get me another one— NOW!"

- Does she think Deanna is being passive, aggressive, or assertive?
- How does she think Deanna's friends and the waiter might respond to her behavior?
- How would she handle this situation?

DILEMMA #2: CONFRONTING A FRIEND WHO IS BEING DISRESPECTFUL

Erica loaned her friend Vicky a sweater she got as a birthday present. When Vicky first asked to borrow it, Erica wanted to say no, since Vicky leaves her own clothes and shoes in big messy piles all over her floor. But Erica said yes, hoping that Vicky would respect the things she has borrowed. A few days later, Erica is at Vicky's house and notices her sweater on the floor under some dirty clothes. Erica feels her stomach getting hot on the inside. She says, "I just remembered I have to be home," and then leaves.

- Does she think Erica is being passive, aggressive, or assertive?
- Does she think Erica and Vicky have a good friend-ship?
- How would she handle this situation?

DILEMMA #3: SETTING LIMITS ON SEXUAL INTIMACY

Clare is watching a movie at home with her boyfriend, Kyle. They've been dating for two months. For the last two weekends, they have been getting more physical with each other. They like to sit really close together when they're watching movies, and sometimes they make out for a long time not paying any attention to the screen. Tonight, they start kissing and then Kyle starts touching Clare's chest and hips. Her body feels good, but things are going too fast and too far for Clare. After only two months of dating, she and Kyle are still just getting to know one another. She looks Kyle in the eyes and says, "I need to stop. Let's take a walk or something. I want to get some air, talk, and figure out what I'm doing here."

- Does she think Clare is being passive, aggressive, or assertive?
- How does she think Kyle should handle this situation?
- How would she handle this situation?

DILEMMA #4: FIGHTING WITH SOMEONE YOU LOVE

Betty spends half the week with her mom and half the week with her dad. Ever since her parents split up six months ago, it's been this way—back and forth. Betty is glad she doesn't have to give either one of them up completely, but it's hard for her. Lately, both of her parents are busy and it seems like they are not listening to her when she tells them things that happened to her during the day. She starts making her stories more interesting, lying about the details and making her life sound more exciting and dangerous than it is. Her dad notices and says, 'Honey—how dumb do you think I am?' Betty feels embarrassed and angry, and she screams, "I think you're REALLY dumb!' Then she runs to her room and slams the door as hard as she can.

- Does she think Betty is being passive, aggressive, or assertive?
- How does she think Betty might be feeling right now?
- How would she handle this situation?

Saying things directly may feel scary or even useless to a girl. If you can see that she is struggling with a conflict, offer to help her talk through all her feelings about the issue. What is she afraid will happen if she speaks up? What does she hope will happen? Does she want to yell and scream and hurt the person who has hurt her?

Let a girl know that feeling aggressive or even violent when she has been hurt is natural and understandable, but she should not act on those violent feelings or wishes. Try to give her ways to express her aggression safely, through intense physical exercise, through writing or drawing, by screaming at the top of her lungs, or by smashing something that's not valuable and without hurting herself or anyone else.

Offer to play the role of the person she needs to confront and practice the interaction until both she—and you—feel confident about how she plans to handle the situation.

Talking About Real Danger

The U.S. Department of Justice characterizes rape as "a crime committed primarily against youth." According to its 1998 findings, about one American woman in five is raped in her lifetime. Among women who have been raped, 22 percent were under age twelve, and 32 percent were between ages twelve and seventeen when they were first raped.

A 1997 Harris Interactive survey on the health of adolescent girls also showed that about one in four girls in grades nine through twelve has been the victim of physical abuse, sexual abuse, or date rape. And about one in eleven girls reported having broken up with a boyfriend because she was afraid he would physically harm her.

How do you discuss real danger with a girl without making her feel like she is a target for victimization? How do you communicate to a girl the importance of paying attention to dangers she may be too young to see or understand? One way to begin is by first considering your own experiences of growing up and facing situations that were scary or harmful.

- What scary situations did you find yourself in as a girl?
- Did you ever stay home alone? How did you feel about that?
- How did you think you would protect yourself in dangerous situations?
- Do you have self-defense skills? How did you learn them?

By describing to a girl your own process of facing your vulnerability to various forms of danger, you can gently lead her through awareness and understanding about important health and safety issues. The most important action you can take in the meantime is to believe a girl when she tells you she is afraid or that she has already been hurt. Your ability to respond to a crisis in a girl's life can make all the difference in the world.

"It was around six o'clock, and everyone except the athletic teams had already gone home from school," says Olivia, a sixteen-year-old from a rural town outside Omaha, Nebraska. "My swim practice had finished about fifteen minutes before, and I was already walking out to my car when I realized I needed this one book from my locker. I had to go back inside.

"As I was going up the stairs to get to my locker on the third floor, I passed some guys from the boys' basketball team coming down. They were just leaving—or so I thought.

"After I got my book, I went down that same stairway, and there they all were, five of them, on the second-floor landing. I felt my skin go cold, but I kept walking down the stairs.

"Basically, they jumped me. It was like a frenzy. I felt two hands on my hips, another one pulled my hair, and then they were all over me, pulling my clothes, feeling me up. They closed in on me, laughing and saying how I should 'stick around, we could have some fun.'

"I screamed, 'Get off of me!' I called them names. I pushed back. But I didn't stand a chance. They managed to pull my sweatshirt all the way off and then they just ran. So I did, too. I don't know how I drove home. I don't remember starting the car or anything.

"The moment my mom saw me come in the door, she got this look on her face. It was weird, like she already sensed what had happened. The next thing I knew she was holding me and rocking me while these horrible sounds were coming out of me. I never cried that hard before. After I calmed down, I told her what happened.

"My mom listened and then told me how something like that happened to her during her first year of college. She was leaving a party when these guys surrounded her, felt her up, said some nasty stuff to her, and then they were gone. It was a total hit and run—for both of us.

"It helped me to hear her say it wasn't my fault, and I had a right to feel as bad as I did. I think that's what gave me the courage to press charges. My principal is a really tough woman, too, and she believed me right away. She said she was not going to tolerate this in her school.

"I know I couldn't have faced what happened if my mom hadn't been behind me all the way. In fact, I don't know what I would have done. Hide, I guess."

Talking about real danger is incredibly difficult, but protecting a girl from harm means telling her the truth about what can and, too often, does happen. Usually, a girl is already attuned to many kinds of danger and violence, and she is relying on the adults in her life to tell her how to cope with it.

According to a 1998 report by the Horatio Alger Association, approximately one in three high school students said that violence and crime were the most important concerns that school-age children face. A 1997 Harris Interactive survey on the health of adolescent girls revealed that about half of the girls surveyed did not always feel safe in the neighborhood where they lived. And a 1997 national summary of girls in grades six through twelve showed that one in four girls reported being afraid another student would hurt her at school.

A Girls Inc. study on the impact of violence on girls revealed that many girls confront violence every day. They said their schools, neighborhoods, and sometimes their homes can be dangerous places for them. Girls are aware of gangs, drugs, and weapons in their schools and communities, and report witnessing incidents of sexual and physical harassment, peer and family violence.

"I have learned firsthand that girls want help dealing with the violence that surrounds them," says Girls Inc. former president Isabel Carter Stewart. "I once attended a meeting at a school for pregnant and parenting teens where girls asserted that 'walking away' is not a viable solution for them, and saying no is not enough.

"Girls ask us to teach them how to be 'street smart.' They want to know who they can call when they need help and where they can go that's safe."

A girl needs to know when and where she feels unsafe in her life, and why. Armed with 'street smarts,' self-defense skills, and a strong sense of her own capabilities, a girl can begin to name the things that frighten her, name the areas in her school or neighborhood where she does not feel safe, and offer her own ideas about how she might avoid danger and harm.

"Girls tell us that there are areas in school and in their neighborhoods that kids control and where girls feel especially unsafe," says Dr. Heather Johnston Nicholson. "Girls are angry at adults for leaving them vulnerable in these areas. We give a girl the opportunity to draw us a map of her school, her neighborhood, and her home, if necessary, and circle every place where she feels afraid, and why. We encourage her to name her fears and then ask the adults in her life: How are you going to help me deal with this?"

A girl who is confident and safe in the world knows her

way around a relationship, a building, a neighborhood, and even a whole city. The next three activities will help you prepare a girl to find her way through or around everything from complicated intimate relationships to empty stairways to new and unfamiliar roads.

Get Out the Map—Part 1

Help a girl create a map of her school and the route she takes to and from school. Ask her to circle anyplace on the map where she feels scared or unsure of herself. There may be certain times of the day when a particular hallway, the locker room, or a specific bathroom is crowded with people whom she experiences as threatening. Ask her how she deals with this now. Ask her if she would like help dealing with this in the future.

She and her friends may have already come up with a great way to get around or past an unpleasant situation. But if she reveals a situation where it sounds as if she and others are being harassed or mistreated, this is your chance to intervene. Speak to her and her friends, other parents, and the principal. Find out what's going on and come up with a solution together.

Get Out the Map—Part 2

Buy a map of the city or town where a girl lives. Look over the map and encourage her to point out the roads and areas she normally travels on and through. Make sure she understands how to read a map and how to determine which way is north, south, east, and west.

If she uses public transportation, look at a map showing all the bus, subway, train, and trolley routes. If the route she usually travels is shut down for some reason unexpectedly, what are her other options? Figure these things out together, acknowledging that getting around can be irritating, and that often the roads, bus, and train schedules are not exact or are not clearly marked. She needs to feel comfortable asking for directions, reading a map, and calling you or some other person if she gets lost.

Knowing the Way

How often does a girl you care about get driven to and from school, piano lessons, the mall, the movies, and her friends' houses? Does she know the way to and from these places? Here's a chance to make sure she does. Next time you have to go to one of these familiar destinations, ask her to navigate, telling you to "turn right here," "make a left at the second stoplight," and so on.

Build in some extra time for this trip so that it's okay if she makes some wrong turns. If she does, help her to reorient herself so that she can find her way back or find a different route. Do this as often as you can to build her confidence, self-reliance, and awareness of her environment.

Self-Defense Is the Best Defense

Self-defense is anything a person does to make herself more safe. Asserting a personal boundary, walking away, running away, kicking, yelling, or telling someone what is happening are all forms of self-defense. When a girl masters the following self-defense skills, she will feel more confident in her ability to address threatening and unfamiliar situations in a strong, smart, and bold way.

Six Stars of Self-Defense

★ STAR #1: GET AWAY

A girl needs to know that she always has the right to leave a dangerous, threatening, or merely unpleasant situation by walking or running away. Encourage her to get in the habit of knowing where all the exits are in a room. Remember to include windows and fire escapes. Ask her to come up with a situation where she would need to know where all the exits are—for example: if there was a fire or if someone in the room was bothering her.

★ STAR #2: USE YOUR VOICE

A girl can use her voice softly, firmly, or loudly to defend herself and her space, and to respect others' space. If she bumps into someone in the lunch line, she can say, "Excuse me" or "I'm sorry." If she can't get loose from another person's grip, she can yell or scream for help. If someone tries to get her to do something she doesn't want to do, she can use the Language of Boundaries she practiced earlier in the chapter. It's important that she look that person in the eyes and let them know she is serious. This is a brave way to be, and may take practice.

★ STAR #3: USE YOUR MIND

A girl's mind is a great self-defense weapon. Let a girl know that if she feels threatened—and is not in any immediate physical danger—she should take a few deep breaths and ask herself calmly, What can I do? She should repeat these words as many times to herself as she needs to until an option or several options present themselves.

★ STAR #4: BLOCKS, HITS, AND KICKS

If a girl really wants to learn how to defend herself in situations that threaten physical danger, help her to find a good self-defense class where she learn blocks, hits, and kicks. If you know any good moves, now's the time to show her.

★ STAR #5: TRUST YOUR FEELINGS

A girl needs to know that the "uh-oh" feeling she gets in the pit of her stomach is there for a reason. Let her know that knots in her stomach, butterflies, chills, a pounding heartbeat, or "a cold sweat" are the body's way of signaling to us that something is wrong. She should always pay attention to these feelings. They can lead her away from danger and let her know when it's time to ask for help or to tell a trusted adult what's going on.

★ STAR #6: HAVE THE COURAGE
   TO TELL

Let a girl know that sometimes the only way to get safe or to stop a bad situation from continuing, and possibly getting worse, is by telling. Let her know you are someone she can depend on. Be specific, but also be honest. If you feel you can handle really bad or scary news, say so. Give her examples of worst-case scenarios you feel sure you can handle (without frightening her).

If there are some scenarios that you know you would have a lot of trouble with, say so. The girl in your life probably already figured this out anyway. Anything she cannot tell you, she needs to be able to share with another trusted adult. Urge her to designate which adults in her life she can rely on for an emergency "telling" situation.

Hurting from the Inside Out

"I want to wake up in the morning and not have anything to worry about," says Mindy, fifteen, from Grand Rapids, Michigan. "My parents yell at me for being too thin and try to scare me into eating more. They took me to a doctor who told me if I don't eat more, I'll get an ulcer. I looked up ulcers on the Internet and you don't even get ulcers from not eating!

"I cut my hair really short and my parents accused me of trying to make myself 'ugly.' I said, 'Thanks for the compliment.' They call my friends losers, and I say just because they don't get all dressed up to go to school doesn't make them losers. My parents and I are getting into more and more arguments. I just want to be free of them. I want to be free of everything."

There are numerous factors that can contribute to a girl's feeling depressed, apathetic, self-destructive, and antisocial. If a girl you care about is showing signs that she needs help coping with the pressures in her life—and she is shutting you out— you need to get additional support for yourself and for her. She may not feel comfortable turning to you, but you can take control of finding someone else with whom she can openly share her problems.

According to the 1997 Commonwealth Fund and Harris Interactive Survey on the health of adolescent girls, about one in four high school girls report depressive symptoms. Girls with symptoms of depression are more likely than girls without these symptoms to smoke, drink, and use drugs.

This same survey also showed that a significant number of girls in grades five through twelve want their doctors to discuss physical abuse, sexual abuse, safety, violence, and incest with them; however, only a small percentage say that their doctors have raised these issues with them. Girls who have been abused are more likely to be embarrassed or uncomfortable discussing these problems with their doctors than girls who have not been abused. And, since the majority of girls report that the abuse happened to them at home, and girls are most likely to be abused by a family member or friends of the family, they often need encouragement from trusted adults outside the family before they can talk about what is going on.

A girl must understand that she is inflicting harm on herself by engaging in such self-destructive patterns or behavior as binge drinking; using drugs; dieting to starvation; abusing diet pills, sleeping pills, caffeine pills, or steroids; inducing vomiting; cutting her skin; getting into fights; having sex when she doesn't want to or when she's drunk or high; having unprotected sex; spending time in areas that are unsafe and where no responsible adults are present; driving drunk or riding with a drunk driver; flirting with or engaging in prostitution; and fantasizing about or attempting suicide.

These actions do not necessarily indicate that a girl is depressed, has a drug or alcohol problem, or has been abused. But they do signal a lack of understanding about the dangers to a girl's health and well-being, as well as an inability to cope with feelings or situations that feel intolerable to her. She needs help, intervention, support, nurturing, understanding, and limits. And so do you.

Let a girl know you are concerned, seek professional help and counseling from someone outside the family and your circle of friends, and keep the lines of communication open between the two of you as much as possible while you work things out. In the meantime, make sure that you have someone you can talk to about your fears, worries, and anger at how she may be acting.

Being safe in the world is a right, not a privilege. A girl with the knowledge to protect and defend herself has the foundation for growing into a healthy and secure woman.

Ways to Empower a Girl to Have Confidence in Herself and to Be Safe in the World

- *Remind a girl that although she can't control how those around her behave, she can sharpen her mind and use her body and her voice to stay as safe as possible.*

- *Show a girl that being polite is not the best way to deal with a person who is acting badly. If someone is bothering her, hurting her feelings or her body, or putting her in danger, she should say so and leave the situation as quickly as she can.*

- *Let a girl know that it is not her fault if she is hurt, tricked, or betrayed, and then give her the skills she can use to avoid these painful experiences in the future.*

- *Teach a girl that she is in charge of her own pleasure and comfort, that she can choose to be held, choose to show affection, choose the kind of play, and choose to be left alone by anyone at anytime. And be an example in honoring her choices.*

- *Make sure a girl knows that it is not her job to make other people feel happy, loved, attractive, or secure. The only person she has to please is herself.*

- *Tell a girl that she is never obliged to kiss someone or to be kissed, to be tickled, to be picked up and held, to be hugged or petted, or to be good-natured when she feels that someone is making fun of her.*

- *Teach a girl that it is not acceptable for someone to get into her space without first asking her for and then getting her permission.*

- *Teach a girl that it is always acceptable for her to say to anyone at any time: "Stop" and "Wait."*

- *Teach a girl the words she can use to assert and protect her boundaries. When you observe her setting a boundary, let her know you are proud of her.*

- *Teach a girl that respecting other people's boundaries and asking them to respect yours builds trust and shows them that you want to have a good relationship.*

- *Pay attention to the way other adults or relatives behave around a girl. If someone acts in a way that feels inappropriate to you, let that person know what bothers you and why.*

- *Acknowledge the emotional cost that comes with speaking up and speaking out against unwanted attention, affection, pressure, or abuse, and give a girl a lot of credit for standing up for herself.*

- *Share your own difficult experiences of standing up to pressure with a girl so she knows that it can be hard for anyone.*

- *Teach a girl how to "fight fair" and how to resolve a conflict without making it worse by being violent and unnecessarily aggressive.*

- *Make room and opportunities for a girl to acknowledge and express her aggression safely.*

- Let a girl know whom she can call when she needs help and where she can go that's safe.

- Teach a girl that asserting a personal boundary, walking away, running away, kicking, yelling, or telling someone what is happening are all forms of self-defense.

- Create opportunities for a girl to learn her way around the town where she lives. Make sure she knows how to read a map and suggest she carry one with her at all times just in case.

- Find out what a girl is afraid of and why. Offer to help her figure out ways to confront this fear without endangering herself.

- Let a girl know that knots in her stomach, butterflies, chills, a pounding heartbeat, or "a cold sweat" are the body's way of signaling to her that something is wrong. She can trust these feelings to lead her away from danger and let her know when it's time to ask for help or to tell a trusted adult what's going on.

- Remind a girl that anything she cannot tell you, she needs to be able to share with another trusted adult. Urge her to designate which adults in her life she can rely on for an emergency "telling" situation.

- Pay attention to how a girl is coping and not coping with the pressures, feelings, relationships, and important events in her life. Let her know what you see, and get help for both of you if the problems or the communication between you become more serious or impossible.

• *Trust your own instincts about what you think may be going on with a girl you care about. If you have a bad feeling in your gut—if you recognize an eating disorder, problems with drugs and alcohol, sexual problems, depression, or indications of any kind of abuse—tell another adult whom you trust and can rely on. Then get outside help for you and the girl you care about.*

6.

Preparing for Economic Independence

*"I believe that all women should have the
right to do what they believe in."*
EBONIE, AGE TWELVE

First, the good news. Girls are no longer sitting around waiting for Prince Charming to come along and sweep them off their feet. *Three out of four girls in a 1998 Girls Inc./Harris Interactive Survey say they do not expect their financial future will be made secure by the person they marry.*

Now, the bad news. Girls worry a great deal about money, and they are nervous and uncertain about how to deal with their finances. The number one concern of girls in a 1998 Yankelovich Partners study is that they will not have enough money at some point in their lives. In addition, girls do not consider themselves as knowledgeable or confident as boys about *financial issues* or managing money, according to the Girls Inc./Harris Interactive Survey.

> *Girls'*
> *Bill of Rights*
> *#6*
>
> Girls have the
> right to prepare
> for interesting
> work and
> economic
> independence.

And the facts support a girl's fears. Although the average woman in the United States works for pay for most of her life, she earns an average of 76 cents for every dollar a man earns. In addition, a woman with a college degree makes less money than a man with a high school education, and a woman with an advanced master's degree earns less than a man who only has a bachelor's degree.

"A girl needs to be know about money, wealth, power, and independence," says Girls. Inc. Director of Research, Dr. Heather Johnston Nicholson. "Three-quarters of working-age women participate in our country's workforce, and, in many cases, they are supporting their children, as well as themselves. In order for a girl to be prepared for economic self-sufficiency, she must learn to be a responsible money manager as well as a savvy investor."

Taking Care of Business

Lillie is only nine but already concerned about money. "I worry about college," she says. "My mom works real hard to take care of me and my brothers, but I'm afraid she won't be able to afford something as expensive as college. I can hardly wait until I'm old enough so I can get a part-time job and begin saving up. My mom tells me that whatever happens, she'll find a way to pay for me but I'm scared it won't be enough."

Unfortunately, Lillie is not alone with her concerns. The Girls Inc./Louis Harris survey found that girls in grades five through nine are extremely anxious about money and are especially troubled about how they'll be able to pay for their college education. They also say that the way they deal with their financial fears is to a great extent determined by what they see at home: 50 percent of the girls cite their mother as the *one* person who has taught them the most about matters relating to money.

Did you have similar worries about your financial security when you were you daughter's age? If so, you're not alone. Three-fourths of all adult women in a 1997 Girls Inc./Oppenheimer Funds survey say they wished they had learned more about money when they were growing up, and only 6 percent now consider themselves very knowledgeable about financial investments.

Think Back

• *What jobs were women expected to do when you were a girl?*

• *What did you want to be when you were your daughter's age?*

• *Did you tell your parents or other important adults about your ambition? If so, how did they respond?*

• *Did you get an allowance or earn money when you were a girl?*

• *Did you spend it or save it?*

• *How would you describe your mother's relationship to money when you were a girl? Did she manage the money your father earned? Was she the sole earner? Did she have her own money?*

• *Would you say your mother was comfortable with money? Why or why not?*

It is essential to break the cycle of uncertainty about money that is passed from one generation to the next. The key to changing this pattern is to give a girl the tools she needs to become an economically independent adult. Every girl should know how to create a budget, track her expenses, open a bank account, use a credit card, buy and sell stocks and bonds, and develop an investment strategy. She can begin by learning to manage the money she gets through an allowance, a job, or for doing chores.

Most girls want to be in charge of their own finances—as do their mothers. According to the Girls Inc./Oppenheimer survey, 79 percent of girls—and 75 percent of women—say they would like to learn more about how to manage and invest money.

"I want both my daughters to be independent and able to live on their own," says Robin, the owner of a boutique in the Los Angeles area. "As a single mother, I'm very conscious of being the sole support for my children. I'm the one who worries about paying for their school, buying their clothes, affording the little—and not so little—extras that are so important when you're growing up. It would be wonderful if my daughters end up eventually sharing their lives with a partner who would help out with some of the financial responsibilities. But, ultimately, I want my girls to be prepared to take care of themselves and, if need be, their own children as well."

In order for a girl to grow up to be financially savvy—and comfortable—she must recognize how money affects her directly, as well as how it impacts on her family and her community. The following activity will help a girl understand the concept of creating a budget, the first basic step in her economic education.

Life on 100 Pennies

You'll need a large sheet of paper or poster board, something to write with, and 100 pennies. If 100 pennies aren't easily accessible, you can use paper clips, or something similar. Explain that the two of you are going to imagine that she's living on her own and is in charge of paying her own expenses. All her needs can be met with an income of 100 pennies a month.

• *Once a girl has gathered all her pennies, help her to think of all the possible expenses that come with living on her own. For example: rent or mortgage, food, clothes, transportation, phone and electric bills, taxes, and don't forget entertainment—everybody deserves a movie now and then, in addition to a few evenings out.*

• *Now have her divide her pennies into stacks to illustrate the different kinds of expenses she'll need to cover. For example, rent is an expense that can cost about 25 percent of a person's income. Help your daughter figure out 25 percent of 100 pennies, and set aside that many pennies for rent. Keep doing this with all other expenses.*

• *After she has divided her money into stacks, have her write down how she decided to spend her income, with the expenses listed in the left column and the amount of money she plans to spend written down in the right. Let her know that what she created is called a budget—the amount of money she has (income), compared to the amount of money she spends (expenses).*

You can take this exercise even further by looking together at the real estate and help wanted sections of the newspaper. Find out how much it costs to rent an apartment or buy a house. Then check out the salary range for positions that appeal to her. Use these figures to create another budget based on actual living expenses (include food, transportation, and so on) and working at a job she considers interesting.

Now that the girl in your life knows how to create a budget, why not include her in paying the bills?

Paying Bills

Next time you sit down to write checks out for monthly bills, ask her to help you. If you have the bills organized and know what the payments will be, let her write out all the checks that you will then sign.

• *Explain how to read a bill. When is the bill due? Can she find your account number on the bill? Who should the check be made out to?*

• *Have her write the numbers of the checks, to whom the check was made out, and what the amount was in your checkbook or wherever you keep this information. Explain why it is important to keep track of all the checks you write.*

- *If your bills are not organized, ask her to help you sort them out according to which ones need to be paid first.*

It's worth both your time and effort to increase a girl's familiarity and skill at handling money. She needs to know that bills are not something that you can or need to hide from. With this routine exposure to the expenses in running a household, she will be better prepared to take charge of her own finances and deal with money more comfortably and responsibly in the future.

Girl Power

"Kimberly knows the designer labels better than I do," explains Helene, a landscape architect from Cleveland. "My stepsister is only seven but already distinguishes between brand names, different stores, and distinct styles. I know her tastes are influenced by the programs she watches on television but there's also this incredible pressure among her friends to look fashionable. I want her to be smart about shopping but I don't want her to become obsessed with spending all her money on clothes. I really don't know where to draw the line."

There are now 16 million girls in the United States between the ages of seven and fourteen, with access to $100 billion in spending power, and they represent a market that is growing in both numbers and potential.

"Girls have emerged as a prime target for companies from camera makers to entertainment conglomerates," according to

The New York Times. "There is now a $5 billion-a-year market in preadolescent girls' clothing. In addition, two-thirds of these girls have access to a computer, making them a potential source for online purchases."

Girls as young as four years old are being targeted by the fashion industry, and they in turn are developing specific tastes and preferences. "We are seeing the deliberate teening of childhood," believes Kay Hymowitz, author of *Ready or Not: Why Treating Children as Small Adults Endangers Their Future—and Ours.* "Now, parents are giving their kids a lot more choices on what to wear at ever younger ages. The advertisers know this and they are exploiting the kids' longing to seem sophisticated and grown up. One result is a loss of a precious period of independence from conformity."

The 1998 Roper Youth Report found that more girls than boys start out aware of the consumer market and its myriad of choices. Six-year-old girls are twice as likely as boys to choose their own toys and games, and one and a half times as likely to choose their own books. These differences don't change over time: the study also found that girls between the ages of fifteen and seventeen are twice as likely as boys in their age group to have a credit card.

Learning to be a responsible consumer is also a major part of economic self-sufficiency. You should help a girl understand that she has the right to choose wisely and to buy only what she can afford. The following activity illustrates the importance of her making smart purchases and getting the most for her money, and involves a trip to her favorite store or the local shopping mall.

Power Shopping

A girl might find it fun to ask some of her friends to join her in this quest to become a power shopper.

- *Have her and her friends pretend they have $500 to buy the items they want for their school wardrobe. Their mission is to get as many items as possible with this amount of money. How many outfits can they buy? What about accessories such as jewelry, barrettes, or combs for their hair? A purse or a backpack? Makeup, if appropriate?*

- *Each girl should take a piece of paper and fold it in half. On one side, she should write Cost of Item I Bought and Designer? Yes or No; on the other side, Cost of Item I Didn't Buy and Designer? Yes or No.*

- *Accompany the girls to the shopping center or mall if they're not old enough to go themselves. Tell them to be sure to compare prices before they "buy" because they may find what they want in another store for less money. Also, point out that an item may be more expensive if it comes from a particular designer or if it's sold in a fancy store.*

- *The girls should keep track of their "purchases," at the same time carefully noting down the items they choose not to buy. At the end of the exercise, they should total up both sides and see how much money they've saved by being a power shopper.*

- *Ask the girls to consider if they were able to buy as much with $500 as they thought. What were some of the differences between the lower-and higher-priced items (quality, color, how well the items fit)?*

What would make them buy an item for a higher price? What was most important to them when looking for a particular item?

• *Ask them how much their friends, classmates, movies, television, and magazines influence what they want to buy and how much they're willing to spend on their appearance.*

Purchasing is a responsibility as well a means of empowerment.Once a girl understand she can save money in the long run by deciding what she wants and needs most—and sticking to it—she can begin to make thoughtful decisions about how much she spends and what she buys.

Equal Pay for Equal Work

"Technology, science, math, and computers are not words usually associated with women and girls," says Brenda Stegall, director of training at Girls Inc. "Even though there's a perception out there that a girl will not be able to perform as well in science or math or computers regardless of her demonstrated abilities, our experience is just the opposite: a girl will jump at the opportunity to enter these fields if given the chance. A girl who is supported by adults instead of protected by them—in any arena—learns to embrace her curiosity, face her fears, and trust her own judgment."

Although the majority of working-age women participate in the workforce, many of them are clustered in lower-paying occupations and are underrepresented in fields requiring professional skills. The following activity explores different job and career options, and provides an opportunity to discuss how a girl's hobbies and interests might connect her to a future career.

Career Charades or What's My Line?

Think back to when you were seven. Ask yourself:

- Did you know what your mother did for work?
- Did you know what her hobbies or special interests were?
- What jobs did you think women did?
- How did this knowledge influence what you wanted to do or be when you grew up?

Now think of a girl you care about. Ask yourself:

- Does she know and understand what you do for work?
- Does she know what your hobbies and special interests are?
- What jobs does she think women do?
- Has she talked about what she wants to do or be when she grows up?
- Does she have some hobbies or special interests that could be relevant to a particular job or career area?

Before starting:

- Ask a girl what she wants to be when she grows up.
- Ask her if she knows what you do each day and why. Then explain to her what you actually do.

• Share with her the information that women work in all kinds of jobs and careers, and encourage her to name some of them with you. You can also spend time looking through magazines with her to see how women are portrayed in work situations.

Rules of the game:

• You each take a turn thinking of a job or career. Make sure that when it's your turn, you try to name some nontraditional choices.
• Using words, sentences, or phrases, describe what tasks are involved in that job or career, what equipment might be used in it, whether it's performed indoors or outdoors, and so on.
• You cannot name anyone who actually is engaged in that job or career.
• When one of you guesses correctly, it's the other person's turn.

Consider whether or not a particular job interests either of you. Why is it appealing? Discuss how her hobbies and special interests would be valued in a particular line of work. Explore different ways she can apply her skills and knowledge in her potential career.

The work world is wide open now, and a girl should be aware that it's hers for the taking. Familiarize her with as many career choices as possible at the earliest age possible. The United States has one of the highest female labor force participation rates among the industrialized countries, and the distinction between *traditional* and *nontraditional* jobs for women is beginning to blur. There are now more women than ever before who are doctors, lawyers, engineers, construction workers, small business owners, elected officials, investment bankers, computer programmers—and the list goes on.

"I believe that women and men have the same opportunities in their lives," asserts Penny, a ninth grader from Salt Lake City. "We just have to go after them the same way. I love science and am planning to be a geologist. I also want to be financially independent so I can take care of myself and not depend on others. My mother is always complaining about her work. She says she's sorry she didn't study to be an architect, that she wishes she had a more interesting job. I don't want to be bored at what I'm doing, that's the key. I also plan to get married but I don't see how one thing affects the other."

Most girls take it for granted that they will work when they grow up. They also consider their career options unlimited. Indeed, according to the Girls' Rights Survey, nearly two-thirds of girls say they do not experience stereotypes that interfere with their right to prepare for interesting work and economic independence.

"As adults, we should be constantly encouraging girls to bump themselves up a notch," advises Girls Inc. Director of Program Development, Jan Stanton. "Even an activity such as cooking with your daughter can involve math, science, and technology. Ask your daughter if she knows what microwaving is all about. Discuss how nutritionists measure caloric intake to create healthy diets. Use measurements to compare the metric system with ours. Then, enjoy together the best brownies ever!"

Today, technological literacy is essential for any kind of professional endeavor a girl ultimately enters. The reality is clear: unless a girl acquires the skills she needs to succeed in the information age, she will be relegated to the bottom of the pay scale. A girl must be encouraged to start with computers and become part of the Internet's virtual community at an early age. She should also be introduced to different careers in technology and new media so she does not end up on the wrong side of the digital divide.

According to the U.S. Department of Labor, careers in computer science and systems analysis are expected to grow faster than any other occupation over the next several years. And girls are eager to be part of these new information networks: 60 percent of girls in a 1997 Gallup Organization study say they want to learn more about technology and computer advances such as faster processing chips and more sophisticated software. In addition, nearly equal proportions of girls and boys said they have high confidence in their computer skills.

"Close to a quarter of a million girls across the country are currently being trained by Girls Inc. to improve their technological skills and knowledge," explains Ms. Stanton. "They love working on the computer. They're also very aware of the terrific job opportunities in this field, in terms of salary, job security, and flexibility in work hours."

Women now are also experiencing great success as entrepreneurs and small business owners. The U.S. Small Business Administration reports that there were approximately eight million women business owners in 1996, with their businesses employing nearly 20 million people and generating more than $2.3 trillion in sales. In addition, the number of women business owners increased by 78 percent between 1992 and 1996.

Starting your own business requires careful planning and organization. The following activity encourages a girl's entrepreneurial spirit by helping her develop a business plan and strategy for her own company.

The Sandwich Maker

Explain that in order for a girl to succeed as an entrepreneur, she will have to work hard to make her product the most sought after in the market. The product in this activity is sandwiches and she will be starting her own sandwich-making business.

• *Ask her: What is her favorite sandwich? What are the ingredients (peanut butter, pickles, mayonnaise, mustard, tomatoes, turkey, lettuce, cheese, etc.)?*

• *Tell her to imagine that everyone in her community loves the same sandwich as she does. Since she likes making (and eating) that particular sandwich, she is in the perfect position to provide something that is needed in her community: a business that makes everyone's favorite sandwich.*

• *Assist her in developing a plan for her new business by using the following questions as a guide:*

 1. *What makes her sandwiches special and unique? Why would people want to buy them?*

2. *Where would she sell her sandwiches? Would she sell them from home, create her own sandwich stand, or take orders over the phone and deliver them to people's houses and offices?*

3. *How much will it cost her to make her sandwich? For example, let's say she buys one jar of mustard, two bags of rolls, two pounds of cheese, a head of lettuce, three big tomatoes, and two pounds of sliced turkey. Then she makes twelve sandwiches using all those ingredients. Have her divide the total amount she spends for all the ingredients by twelve. The answer she gets will be the cost per sandwich.*

4. *What price would she charge people to buy her sandwich so that she could make a profit? Explain to her that profit is the difference between what it costs to make her sandwich and how much she will charge a person to buy her sandwich. The profit is the amount she gets to keep. She should consider the time it takes her to make the sandwich when figuring out how much to charge. This is what the phrase "time is money" means. Something that takes a long time to make will usually cost more.*

5. *What would she call her sandwich-making business?*

6. *How would she let people know about her sandwiches? Create a Web site together for her business, plan an advertising campaign in the local newspaper, think up a billboard or television commercial.*

A girl deserves an equitable chance to fulfill her career aspirations, whether her plans include starting her own business or becoming a firefighter or studying astrophysics or designing computer software. Only by understanding and mastering the economic realities in her life can a girl be a full and equal participant in our increasingly global society.

Investing in the Future

It took a particularly long and nasty divorce for Donna, an events planner from New Haven, Connecticut, to get over her reluctance to jump into the financial water.

"My ex-husband was in charge of our investment portfolio," she explains, "and I just went along with whatever he decided. Even though I paid all our bills and took care of the household expenses, he chose our stocks and bonds, our pension and retirement plans, even our insurance policies. After my separation, my lawyer suggested I hire a financial advisor. I have to admit that I was shocked and somewhat ashamed about how little I knew about what my husband and I possessed, what we owed, what was ours, and what was his alone. All I knew was that he would always give me financial papers to sign—including our tax returns—and I would do as I was told. I didn't even look them over!

"I suffered enormous financial losses as a result of my divorce. What really bothers me is that I was an economics major in college and was always very good in math. But I just followed my mother's lead and accepted the idea that while a wife's job was to handle the phone bills and pay for the groceries, the man of the house should be in charge of the 'real' money. I abdicated my financial responsibilities and it was a very costly mistake."

Donna explains that she decided to enroll in an adult education course in basic investing. Not only that, she persuaded her sixteen-year-old daughter to join her. "I want Holly to feel comfortable with money and be in control of her own finances," Donna says. "Financial planning is not a man's thing, it's survival. By handing it over, you give up power. It really doesn't make any sense."

According to the Girls Inc./Oppenheimer survey, one-third of women who do not invest their money say their reason is lack of knowledge about the subject. In addition, the study found that one in seven women has no retirement account, and that one in three women with both a retirement account and credit cards owes more on her credit cards than she has in her retirement account.

The good news is that women don't want to pass on their state of financial unenlightenment to their daughters. An overwhelming majority in the survey—87 percent—indicated that they would be interested in having their daughters attend a course on money management and investment.

"Holly told me that she's now considering a career in finance," Donna says proudly. "Once the mystery is taken out of money, it can be a lot of fun. Why should the guys be the only ones playing the game?"

The following activity introduces a girl to the concept of

investing. You will need a copy of the business section of your local newspaper or the *Wall Street Journal*.

Wall Street and My Street

Looking at the stock exchange tables, ask a girl to choose a company from among the various companies that make products she uses every day. For example: the brand of shoes she wears, the kind of computer or television she has, her favorite restaurant chain, or brand of food she likes.

Explain to her that most of the companies that make the clothing she wears, foods she eats, and items she uses every day sell partial ownership of their companies, in the form of "stock" on Wall Street in New York City. Wall Street is the place where stock is bought, sold, and traded. Stock is sold as individual "shares," so that when she owns stock in a company, she will be a shareholder or an investor in that particular company.

As a shareholder in a company, she will make money if the company is successful, because she owns a share of the profit. She'll lose money if the company is not successful, because she owns a share of their losses. She must purchase stock directly from the company or through a stockbroker.

A lot of companies sell their stock over the Internet, and you can research companies together on the Web and also explore on-line investment opportunities. For example, on AOL and other sites, you can create your own stock portfolios that automatically give you the latest share prices and compute your gains and losses for you.

Help a girl find the price of one share in a company she chooses. Follow her stock with her every day, to see if it goes up or down. Estimate how much she would be making—or losing—and explore the possibility of "selling" her present stock in order to "buy" another one. It's fun to make dummy portfolios, filled with stocks of companies you find interesting and potentially profitable.

The next time a girl in your life eats at McDonald's, point out that any investor who bought 100 shares of McDonald's stock for $2,250 in 1965 has seen the value of those shares multiply to nearly $1.8 million!

Money management and financial investing is a fundamental part of a girl's education. Economic literacy is essential in the education of every girl today so she can grow up strong, smart, bold, and economically self-sufficient. A girl must be provided with real-world knowledge and skills, and learn to earn, save, invest, spend wisely. By taking charge of her financial destiny, she is taking care of herself.

Ways to Empower a Girl to Prepare for Interesting Work and Economic Independence

- *Debunk the myth of Prince Charming. Teach a girl that most women will work for pay for most of their lives and every girl needs to be prepared to support herself.*

- *Share with a girl how you first learned about money, and teach her about what you wish you had learned.*

- *Discuss family finances openly. Show a girl that financial planning is part of everyday life, and talk about your income, expenses, and family budget with her.*

- *Counteract the pressure on a girl to ask for less and be satisfied with what she gets. Teach a girl the importance of being paid well for something you do well.*

- *Provide opportunities for a girl to develop interests and skills that can lead to careers in nontraditional fields.*

- *Give a girl the chance to explore her skills and capabilities in science, math, and technology.*

- *Make sure a girl has equal access and time to work on computers, use the Internet, and explore other high-tech equipment in her school and at home.*

- *Develop a network of working women to supplement the career guidance efforts of a girl's school.*

- *Support programs that cultivate girls' job skills and career planning.*

- *Arrange for a girl to visit a firm in the financial sector of your town and have her speak with the women who work there.*

- *Work to achieve comparable pay among women and men for work of comparable value.*

- *Lobby for legislation to make career and family a survivable combination.*

- *Mentor a girl or young woman entering your professional field.*

- *Support and vote for candidates for public office who advocate equal opportunity for girls and women.*

- *Set an example. By respecting yourself and others, you set a standard that a girl can follow.*

Conclusion

Creating an Equitable Society

"I know that I bring something of value to what I do. I plan to work hard, be true to myself, and be treated as an equal in my life."
KELLY, AGE SEVENTEEN

A girl who has complete access to her rights is empowered, not limited, by the fact that she is female.

A girl who exercises her rights can make concrete improvements in her life, at school, at home, and in her community.

A girl who knows how to assert her rights can help ensure that others also have a fair chance at success and happiness.

"Our challenge is to help a girl set higher expectations for herself yet still capture her imagination about being female," says Girls Inc. former president Isabel Carter Stewart. "There is often a 'dumbing down' of girls, which leads them to question their abilities, their value, and their ultimate worth. We must inspire a girl to take charge of her life and back it up with skills, support, and guidance. A girl must also be shown the importance of being supportive of other girls and accepting of others' differences."

When a girl changes her expectations for herself, she also changes and challenges our own ideas: by opening up her world, we open our own. A girl with the tools and self-confidence to navigate her own way can make a difference for herself and others, and work to create an equitable society.

With change, however, come new questions about how to give a girl the room and encouragement she needs to be self-reliant while still looking out for her best interests and safety. In a culture that rewards girls for looking, acting, and spending money like grown-up women, how do you strike a balance between teaching the girl you care about to advocate for herself while also protecting her right to grow up at her own pace?

Many parents and concerned adults are confused about how to deal with the tough decisions regarding raising a girl in today's society: Is it better to buy your ten-year-old daughter a halter top or have her teased by her peers for not being "cool"? Should you criticize your niece for piercing her nose, even when she explains that "everyone else in her class" has also done it? Do you interfere when your daughter's boyfriend doesn't get up from the dinner table to help her clear the dishes?

The answers are not always clear and depend on the individual girl—what she wants, how she expresses her needs, and how she relates to her environment.

"I am in awe of my three granddaughters," says Hannah, a retired art teacher living in Madison, Wisconsin. "They are so confident, so surefooted, so radiantly female. I was raised in the fifties with all those rules about what a girl could and couldn't do. It has taken me this long just to get that out of my system and start seeing myself and the world as if women really do matter. But I have to tell you, some things have not changed a bit since I was a girl.

"I was watching my eight-year-old granddaughter, Annabelle, play with her friend Matt the other day at a family picnic. Now, you have to understand, Annabelle is very outgoing and always in charge of everything. She even tries to tell her mother what to do—which I secretly enjoy since my daughter put me through the same thing!

"Annabelle and Matt were building a fortress out of cardboard boxes in the garage, preparing for some kind of war they dreamed up, and I was sitting nearby in a lawn chair just observing.

"While they were assembling the structure, it was a team effort. Both Annabelle and Matt lifted the boxes and then arranged them together after much consultation. But as soon as they were done building, Matt turned to Annabelle and said, 'I'm going out to search the grounds for signs that the enemy troops are near. You stay here and clean up.'

"My jaw dropped. First of all, there's a war going on and the place needs to be clean? The worst part is Annabelle responded with 'Sure, right away.' And then she ran off to find a broom so she could start sweeping up.

"I wanted to scream. And, of course, I know they were only playing and it's not my business what games Annabelle plays. But I thought to myself, 'When will it end?' Women have got to stop investing our energies in someone else's mission in life and start concentrating on our own. Leave the floor dirty—go find those troops!"

It can be frustrating to see a girl acting in ways that do not seem strong, smart, or bold to us. Fortunately, there is no rule that says every empowered girl must apply the same approach to her life and success. The last thing a girl needs is another set of expectations that does not feel authentic or relevant to her personality. While it is important to notice how a girl responds to those around her, her happiness and success do not depend on her being in charge of every situation. Real empowerment can withstand contradictions and complexities that are a part of a person's individuality.

"The best way to inspire a girl to be strong, smart, and bold is to help her think through her options and decide what she wants," adds Ms. Stewart. "Our investment is in making sure that when a girl runs up against the status quo and is told 'Girls can't do that' or 'Women aren't built for that' she will come back with, 'Oh yeah?' and then do it anyway—her way."

What does your daughter, your granddaughter, your niece, your mentee, or any other girl you care about envision for her future? She probably fantasizes about where she will live, the kind of house or apartment she'll have, the kind of career she wants to pursue, and whether she will get married and have her own family. The following activity is a way to fuel her wildest imagination about what the future may hold for her.

My Future

• *Ask a girl to name four places where she might one day like to live. Encourage her to choose at least one city outside the state where she currently lives, and at least one city outside the country where she lives.*

- *Have her list four kinds of residences she would like to live in. Encourage her to be as imaginative and descriptive as possible. For instance, if she loves being near water, she may choose a houseboat as one of her options. If she is particularly adventurous and loves the outdoors, she may choose to live in a cabin she and her friends build together deep in the woods. If she wants to live in an apartment, ask how many rooms it has. Does it have a porch or a balcony? Does she want a large or small kitchen? Does she want a house big enough that she can put an air hockey table in the basement, build a dance floor, and hang a disco ball from the ceiling? The more specific she can be, the better.*

- *Have her list four different kinds of careers that appeal to her. If she chooses something nonspecific such as scientist, help her to explore what kind of scientist. Does she want to find a cure for a certain disease, study a particular kind of animal, explore the healing properties of plants? If she gravitates more toward traditionally lower-paying and emotionally demanding careers such as social worker, teacher, nurse, or activist, encourage her to choose at least one career that may seem outlandish and extravagant. For example, owner of a casino, the person who takes care of the sharks at the aquarium, or a country and western singer.*

- *Have her describe four different kinds of family arrangements that appeal to her. Use this occasion to teach a girl that a family should provide comfort, a genuine feeling of safety and security, love, good company, quiet solitude, and plenty of opportunities to keep growing and having fun. Assure a girl that, beyond meeting these basic criteria, a family can be whatever she wants it to be. Family can be her and her dog; family can be her and her friends; family can be her and a partner, with kids or without kids; family can be her and a spectacular view of the mountains. In doing so, you help to relieve some of the immense pressure on a girl to get married, have kids, grow old . . . the end. There's room for more. Encourage a girl to take it.*

· *Finally, ask a girl what kind of world she would like to live in. How are decisions made in that world? What are the laws of that world and how are they enforced? Is there anything about the world as she sees and experiences it now that she would like to change? What can she do individually to bring about the kind of change that she desires? What can she do with the help of others who believe in her vision? What can others do to share in making the world a more equitable, friendly, and interesting place?*

· *She may want to write down her answers, then mix and match careers, locations, and families based on what futures go together best. She may also want to create a collage of her possible futures, using images from magazines and travel brochures. She may want to paint or draw her futures. Or she may want to keep her list in a safe place as a quiet reminder of what she has to look forward to. This list will be a real treasure someday. Help her to hold on to it.*

A girl's goals and aspirations for the future must be encouraged and nurtured, but they cannot be achieved in a vacuum. "Girls and women have obligations as well as rights," says Elinor Guggenheimer, the prominent activist and advocate who has been working to advance women's rights for the past fifty years. "We can't crack through the glass ceiling alone. If we try, the only thing we'll get is a headache. By joining together we can break the ceiling with greater force. Yet, even when we succeed, our work is not over—we need to help other women and girls cast aside the barriers that stand in the way."

Empowered Woman, Empowered Girl

"I've evolved in that I'm prouder to be a woman now," says Terry, a veterinarian from Concord, New Hampshire, and the mother of two daughters and a son. "I see women as brave and strong, even though I grew up thinking we were literally the 'weaker' sex. Over the years, I have come to know and meet some pretty terrific women who have done some incredible things in their lives. And I don't just mean starting their own software company or leading an archeological dig in Turkey. I mean doing what they believe in, working at what is important to them, and raising their sons and daughters to be self-confident and caring.

"The only way my children will understand that equality benefits everyone is by watching how I live my own life. I try to be open and accessible with them, and as nonjudgmental as possible. I trust them to teach me and enlighten me about the world as they see it. By respecting and encouraging each other's voices, we are growing together both as a family and as separate and distinct individuals."

For girls and women, a tremendous gap still exists between the opportunities to be employable, healthy, and self-assured, and the enormous pressures to please the culture and conform to the expectations that society places on us. It is our responsibility to work together to bring about real and lasting change through our combined strength, knowledge, and courage.

A girl's voice must be honored and valued, and it is up to us to do this. A girl must be given the tools and skills to express herself, and it is up to us to provide them. A girl must be inspired to believe in endless opportunity, and it is up to us to advocate it. And, a girl must be encouraged to understand and exercise her rights freely and fully in order to create an equitable society for herself and others.

Appendix A:

101 Ways to Empower a Girl and Improve Her World

1. Praise a girl for her skills and success, not only for her appearance. Say "you did a terrific job," instead of "you look pretty today."

2. Ask a girl if she wants a truck, a doll, a jewelry box, a chemistry set, a flute, a bass drum, a new dress, some new software, etc. Keep her options open.

3. Make sure that household chores such as caring for younger children, cleaning up, preparing meals, cutting the grass, taking out the garbage, fixing things, etc., are shared equally by girls, boys, men, and women in your home.

4. Try some role reversal at home. Let a girl sit at the head of the table and a boy prepare his favorite meal for the whole family.

5. Watch your language. Get "boys will be boys" and "you know how girls are" out of your vocabulary.

6. Help a girl get beyond the "yuck." If the opportunity presents itself, insist calmly that she hold a snake, play in the mud, and get her hands dirty discovering the world around her.

7. Introduce a girl to dynamic women and men who combine paid work, volunteer work, and family life in innovative ways.

8. Celebrate the accomplishments of women throughout history.

9. Read a girl's textbooks: Are women's contributions included in history, science, and art? If not, talk to the board of education and/or create a committee for change.

10. Confront the widespread notions of female fragility by challenging the view in the media and elsewhere of assertive women as "unfeminine" or destructive.

11. Teach a girl to watch television and movies with a critical eye, discuss what you've seen together, and look for strong, smart women who are not limited to traditional roles.

12. Ask questions and take action if you see something unfair or biased on television. Write a letter to your local station or the producers of the show voicing your objections.

13. Be aware of what a girl is reading and responding to in media and advertising. If she is drawn to sexist stereotypes, ask what appeals to her. Find a way to share your views without judging hers.

14. Write letters to toy and publishing companies that produce toys, books, and materials you feel promote stereotypes about gender.

15. Address sexism in areas where young people are sorted by gender into educational or sports programs based on interests or skills they are "supposed" to have.

16. Work with other parents and teachers to foster nonsexist environments from nursery school on up.

17. Make sure a girl has one place where she feels free to express herself in the ways that appeal to her talents and sensibilities.

18. Pay attention to the values and viewpoints a girl expresses. Let her know what interests you about what she is saying and begin a conversation about why she feels a certain way.

19. Support a girl who is in the process of changing her point of view and help her hold on to views that do not necessarily match the views of her friends or people and institutions in authority.

20. Teach a girl skills that help her to think on her feet, make her points, and defend her positions without apology.

21. Discourage a girl from expressing herself in a tentative, questioning, or approval-seeking manner.

22. Help a girl find ways to express difficult or confusing feelings.

23. Encourage a girl to find ways to express herself honestly with you and with her friends in the interests of building trust.

24. Remind a girl that as long as she is not endangering herself or someone else, it is okay to keep personal information about herself and others private.

25. Share decision-making authority with a girl so her voice has a significant impact on her own life and the lives of others.

26. Create opportunities for a girl to be a leader. Let her choose the activity, make the rules, settle the disputes.

27. Encourage a girl to talk as much as she wants and listen intently to what she says.

28. Suggest that a girl and her friends write, sign, and mail a letter to the mayor, school board, or the editor of the local newspaper about a particular issue they feel is important.

29. Recommend that a girl start a group where she and her friends can discuss their feelings about a problem, offer possible solutions, and create a plan of action.

30. Encourage a girl to organize a "speak out" where she and her friends can express their views on a particular topic to their teachers, members of the media, or the leaders of a neighborhood organization.

31. Suggest that a girl start her own Web site or "zine" (a self-published magazine she fills with her writing, art-work, poetry, and anything else she likes).

32. Assist a girl in her advocacy efforts by helping her raise funds, get to and from meetings, prepare her letters and publications, or simply by standing by and admiring her energy and enthusiasm.

33. Avoid rescuing a girl. Encourage her to make an imper-fect product, to get disheveled and sweaty in pursuit of a goal, and to make big interesting mistakes.

34. Give a girl bragging lessons. For example, take a girl fishing and when she catches a fish, ask her: "That fish was *how* big? You fought that fish for *how* long before you finally landed it?"

35. Encourage a girl to replace the words "I won't" and "I can't" with "I don't know how" and "I'll try."

36. Pay close attention to a girl when she is working on something that is difficult for her. Help her develop the skills and confidence to ask for help and, if necessary, to redirect her energy toward a goal that will make her happier.

37. Teach a girl how to take the time to get more information before she makes a decision.

38. Help a girl gain experience trusting her own judgment and ability to make a decision. If it will not endanger her or someone else, let her make the choice she wants to make, even though you may feel it is the wrong one.

39. When things don't go as planned, encourage a girl to learn from what happened, let herself off the hook, and move on.

40. Help a girl learn to tell the difference between safe risks and unsafe risks by sharing your experiences and asking her about hers.

41. Encourage a girl to ask herself: Could this risk hurt me? Could it hurt other people? If the answer to both is no, this is probably a low risk, and whatever she chooses will be okay, and it may even turn out great!

42. Guide a girl as she learns to identify short- and long-term rewards that come with taking a specific risk.

43. Give a girl lots of support for expressing how she feels about a particular goal, so that she will also feel free to tell you when she's having trouble, or wants to change her mind or her method for reaching that goal.

44. Encourage a girl to ask herself: Is this what I want, or am I just doing this to please other people or to make them mad? Is it worth it?

45. Let a girl know that making her own decisions and wanting to achieve an important goal is something to be really proud of.

46. Teach a girl that it is okay to let success go to her head. Redefine pride as an "attractive" feminine trait.

47. When a girl goofs, tell her she is still wonderful and amazing, and then do something fun together.

48. When a girl does something you consider amazing, tell her—and then shout it from the rooftops.

49. Help a girl develop a healthy body image by teaching and showing her that beauty comes in different sizes, shapes, colors, and abilities.

50. Encourage a girl to develop a personal style that feels comfortable and attractive to her.

51. Give a girl accurate information about her body so that she can take full charge of her health and hygiene.

52. Teach a girl the importance of maintaining an active lifestyle and staying drug and alcohol free so that she can build a strong and healthy body.

53. Discourage a girl from dieting as a means of losing weight or making changes to her appearance. Instead encourage good nutrition, plenty of fun physical activities, and a new style of clothing or haircut.

54. Observe your own relationship to weight and appearance. If you notice that a girl has picked up your own tendencies to be critical of your appearance, acknowledge this openly with her. Create a new common ground where the two of you can help each other appreciate how you look and feel.

55. Discuss stress with a girl while also sharing your experiences of dealing with stressful situations and feelings. Encourage her to explore healthy ways of managing her stress.

56. Teach a girl to critique beauty ideals for girls and women as they are portrayed in television programs, popular songs, movies, books, and magazines.

57. Lobby the fashion industry to expand its definition of beauty by featuring more diverse-looking models.

58. Help a girl explore what she wants from romantic relationships and what she's looking for in a partner. Find a way to offer your insights about healthy relationships without judging her desires.

59. Teach a girl how to communicate clearly with a date or romantic partner about everything from which movie they will see that night to how far she wants to go physically and emotionally in the relationship.

60. Work with a girl to come up with lines and phrases to help her deal with sexual pressures, and practice these responses with her out loud.

61. Counteract the pressure on a girl to feel shame about her body, her sexuality, and her desire to love and be loved. Let a girl know that feelings of pleasure, love, loss, desire, and confusion are a part of everyone's life.

62. Advocate for health and sex education classes that offer accurate information and place equal emphasis on sexual responsibility for both girls and boys.

63. Support teenage pregnancy prevention initiatives in your community.

64. Remind a girl that although she can't control how those around her behave, she can sharpen her mind and use her body and her voice to stay as safe as possible.

65. Show a girl that being polite is not the best way to deal with a person who is acting badly. If someone is bothering her, hurting her feelings or her body, or putting her in danger, she should say so and leave the situation as quickly as she can.

66. Let a girl know that it is not her fault if she is hurt, tricked, or betrayed, and then give her the skills she can use to avoid these painful experiences in the future.

67. Teach a girl that she is in charge of her own pleasure and comfort, that she can choose to be held, choose to show affection, choose the kind of play, and choose to be left alone by anyone at anytime. And be an example in honoring her choices.

68. Make sure a girl knows that it is not her job to make other people feel happy, loved, attractive, or secure. The only person she has to please is herself.

69. Tell a girl that she is never obliged to kiss someone or to be kissed, to be tickled, to be picked up and held, to be

hugged or petted, or to be good-natured when she feels that someone is making fun of her.

70. Teach a girl that it is not acceptable for someone to get into her space without first asking her for and then getting her permission.

71. Teach a girl that it is *always* acceptable for her to say to anyone at any time: "Stop" and "Wait."

72. Teach a girl the words she can use to assert and protect her boundaries. When you observe her setting a boundary, let her know you are proud of her.

73. Teach a girl that respecting other people's boundaries and asking them to respect yours builds trust and shows them that you want to have a good relationship.

74. Pay attention to the way other adults or relatives behave around a girl. If someone acts in a way that feels inappropriate to you, let that person know what bothers you and why.

75. Acknowledge the emotional cost that comes with speaking up and speaking out against unwanted attention, affection, pressure, or abuse, and give a girl a lot of credit for standing up for herself.

76. Share your own difficult experiences of standing up to pressure with a girl so she knows that it can be hard for anyone.

77. Teach a girl how to "fight fair" and how to resolve a conflict without making it worse by being violent and unnecessarily aggressive.

78. Make room and opportunities for a girl to acknowledge and express her aggression safely.

79. Let a girl know whom she can call when she needs help and where she can go that's safe.

80. Teach a girl that asserting a personal boundary, walking away, running away, kicking, yelling, or telling someone what is happening are all forms of self-defense.

81. Create opportunities for a girl to learn her way around the town where she lives. Make sure she knows how to read a map and suggest she carry one with her at all times just in case.

82. Find out what a girl is afraid of and why. Offer to help her figure out ways to confront this fear without endangering herself.

83. Let a girl know that knots in her stomach, butterflies, chills, a pounding heartbeat, or "a cold sweat" are the body's way of signaling to her that something is wrong.

She can trust these feelings to lead her away from danger and let her know when it's time to ask for help or to tell a trusted adult what's going on.

84. Remind a girl that anything she cannot tell you, she needs to be able to share with another trusted adult. Urge her to designate which adults in her life she can rely on for an emergency "telling" situation.

85. Pay attention to how a girl is coping and not coping with the pressures, feelings, relationships, and important events in her life. Let her know what you see, and get help for both of you if the problems or the communication between you become more serious or impossible.

86. Trust your own instincts about what you think may be going on with a girl you care about. If you have a bad feeling in your gut—if you recognize an eating disorder, problems with drugs and alcohol, sexual problems, depression, or indications of any kind of abuse—tell another adult whom you trust and can rely on. Then get outside help for you and the girl you care about.

87. Debunk the myth of Prince Charming. Teach a girl that most women will work for pay for most of their lives and every girl needs to be prepared to support herself.

88. Share with a girl how you first learned about money, and teach her about what you *wish* you had learned.

89. Discuss family finances openly. Show a girl that financial planning is part of everyday life, and talk about your income, expenses, and family budget with her.

90. Counteract the pressure on a girl to ask for less and be satisfied with what she gets. Teach a girl the importance of being paid well for something you do well.

91. Provide opportunities for a girl to develop interests and skills that can lead to careers in nontraditional fields.

92. Give a girl the chance to explore her skills and capabilities in science, math, and technology.

93. Make sure a girl has equal access and time to work on computers, use the Internet, and explore other high-tech equipment in her school and at home.

94. Develop a network of working women to supplement the career guidance efforts of a girl's school.

95. Support programs that cultivate girls' job skills and career planning.

96. Arrange for a girl to visit a firm in the financial sector of your town and have her speak with the women who work there.

97. Work to achieve comparable pay among women and men for work of comparable value.

98. Lobby for legislation to make career and family a surviv-able combination.

99. Mentor a girl or young woman entering your profes-sional field.

100. Support and vote for candidates for public office who advocate equal opportunity for girls and women.

101. Set an example. By respecting yourself and others, you set a standard that a girl can follow.

Appendix B:

Resource Directory
for Girls

GIRLS INC. NATIONAL HEADQUARTERS
120 Wall Street
New York, NY 10005
212-509-2000
www.girlsinc.org

GIRLS INC. NATIONAL RESOURCE CENTER
441 West Michigan Street
Indianapolis, IN 46202
1-800-374-GIRL (4475)

Girls Inc. Programs

Girls Inc. programs are offered through a network of official Girls Inc. affiliates and program partners across the United States. Trained, professional staff at 130 independent Girls

Inc. organizations work with girls ages six to eighteen at over 1,000 sites, including schools, community centers, and religious institutions. Below is a list of national Girls Inc. programs that are inspiring girls nationwide to be strong, smart, and bold.

- *Discovery—a leadership program that engages girls and women in a particular community to work as partners on an important issue chosen by girls, such as creating safer neighborhoods or improving the social and entertainment opportunities available to young people. Girls build their skills at communication, negotiation, planning, and follow-through together with women who respect and nurture the girls' ideas, creativity, and natural leadership ability.*

- *Eureka—a leadership and adventure program that invites girls to a nearby college campus two summers in a row for four weeks of intensive study. Girls delve into math, science, computers, sports, and careers, and follow-up sessions throughout the school year keep girls engaged in pursuing their educational, athletic, and career goals. A paid internship placement the third and final summer of the program gives girls a chance to apply what they have learned in a professional setting.*

- *Friendly PEERsuasion—a substance abuse prevention program that uses role-playing, decision-making strategies, and peer leadership to educate girls and boys about the harmful physical and emotional effects of substance abuse. Girls learn and teach others how to communicate directly, how to deal effectively with pressure and stress, and how to recognize and resist the appeal of media images that glamorize drinking, smoking, and using drugs.*

- *Girls Dig It—an after-school and summer archaeology program that creates opportunities for girls to study culture and heritage, and to explore questions about how people and societies are shaped. Girls learn to apply the scientific and interpretive methods used in history, anthropology, linguistics, philosophy, and folklore, and gain exposure to a range of careers in these disciplines.*

- *Girls Re-Cast TV—a media literacy program that teaches girls how to analyze media images by comparing and contrasting these images with their lives and the people they know. Girls begin to shape their own opinions about the images that surround them and express those ideas by writing their own TV shows, starting their own publications, and voicing their preferences to entertainment and advertising executives through letters and face-to-face meetings.*

- *Operation SMART (Science, Math, and Relevant Technology)—a hands-on math, science, and technology program that motivates girls to embrace their curiosity as they discover the world around them, by taking risks, getting dirty, and making mistakes in the pursuit of knowledge and adventure. Girls learn to make mechanical repairs to bikes, computers, and other objects that they use every day, hone their skills in math and science, and gain exposure to nontraditional, highly technical, and high-paying careers.*

- *Preventing Adolescent Pregnancy—a comprehensive approach to pregnancy prevention that provides girls with accurate information about sexuality and staying healthy and safe. Girls hone their decision-making abilities through role-playing and dilemmas and learn to assert their boundaries as well as their desires. Girls also identify ways and reasons to avoid early pregnancy and exposure to sexually transmitted diseases, while taking charge of forming relationships with their local health care providers. Girls Inc. applies a start early, stay late approach by offering age-appropriate program components to girls from age nine to eighteen.*

- *Project BOLD—a conflict resolution, violence prevention, and violence reduction program that teaches girls how to cope with and address the violence that surrounds them. Girls learn how to use their minds, their voices, and their bodies to set boundaries and keep themselves as safe as possible. Girls also begin to identify areas in their schools, communities, and homes where they do not feel safe, and work together with adults to improve their safety and self-confidence in any environment.*

- *She's on the Money—a money management program that introduces girls as young as age six to basic financial concepts. Girls practice creating a budget and learn how to earn, spend, save, and invest money wisely. Girls also learn how money influences their world and how they can influence local communities and economies, while gaining exposure to range of careers in the financial services industry.*

- *Sporting Chance—a program that introduces girls to various forms of physical fitness, movement, dance, and individual and team sports. Girls learn the health benefits of physical activity and exertion, build their strength, and experience healthy competition and teamwork. Girls also have the opportunity to pursue sports and adventures such as rock climbing, martial arts, and white-water rafting.*

Girls Inc. Resource Material

Girls' Bill of Rights Poster (free). To order, call the Girls Inc. National Resource Center, 800-374-4475.

Girls' Rights Action Kit. Individual, interactive, and group activities to teach girls to understand and assert their rights, $10.00. Girls Inc. National Resource Center, 800-374-4475.

Money Matters: An Economic Literacy Action Kit For Girls. Individual, interactive, and group activities to teach girls money management skills, $10.00, Girls Inc. National Resource Center, 800-374-4475.

Past the Pink and Blue Predicament: Freeing the Next Generation From Sex Stereotypes. Reviews and summarizes research about gender and discusses ways that girls and boys differs and ways they do not, $2.00, Girls Inc. National Resource Center, 800-374-4475.

Organizations

Center for Research on Women, Wellesley College, 617-283-2502

Consortium for Educational Equity, Rutgers University, 908-932-2071

Educational Equity Concepts, 212-725-1803

National Association for Girls and Women in Sports, 703-476-3450

National Women's History Project, 703-838-6000

Women's Educational Equity Act (WEEA) Publishing Center, 800-225-3088

Web Pages

www.girlsinc.org—home page of Girls Incorporated.

www.anincomeofherown.com—Independent Means, the leading provider of educational financial products and services for girls, offers girls information on money management and networking with mentors on their Web site.

www.daughtersnewsletter.com—Web site of *Daughters* Newsletter.

www.msfoundation.org—Web site for Take Our Daughters to Work Day, includes information for parents, schools, employers, and girls on how to organize an event, as well as facts on girls, school, health, and women in the work world.

www.ncrw.org—Web site of the National Council for Research on Women (NCRW), which connects organizations focused on research, policy analysis, advocacy, and innovative programming on behalf of women and girls.

http://lcweb.loc.gov/rr/mss/guide/women.html—An illustrated guide to the U.S. Library of Congress manuscripts relating to women's history.

Appendix C:

References

American Association of University Women, Educational Foundation. *Shortchanging Girls, Shortchanging America*, 1990.

Brumberg, Joan. *The Body Project: An Intimate History of American Girls.* Vintage Books, 1999.

Commonwealth Fund and Louis Harris and Associates. "The Commonwealth Fund Survey of the Health of Adolescent Girls." 1997.

Crain's New York Business. "Tweenyshoppers: Retailers Recognize Power of Youth." June 5, 2000.

Fennema, Elizabeth. *Justice, Equity and Mathematics Education.* Teachers College Press, Columbia University, 1990.

Gallup Organization. "Teens and Technology." 1997.

Gilligan, Carol. *In a Different Voice: Psychological Theory and Women's Development.* Harvard University Press, 1993.

Girls Inc. and the YWCA of Minneapolis. "Discovery: A Leadership Program for Girls and Women." 1997.

Girls Inc. "Growing Together: A Sexuality Education Program for Girls and Their Parents." 1998.

Girls Inc. "Past the Pink and Blue Predicament: Freeing the Next Generation from Sex Stereotypes." 1992.

Girls Inc. Program Planning Guide. 1993.

Girls Inc. "Responding to the Impact of Violence on Girls: A Community Needs Assessment," 1995.

Girls Inc. "What's Equal: Figuring Out Works for Girls in Coed Settings." 1993.

Girls Inc. "Will Power/Won't Power: Preventing Adolescent Pregnancy." 1998.

Harris Interactive Inc. "Taking the Lead: Girls' Rights in the 21st Century." Girls Inc., 2000.

Henry J. Kaiser Family Foundation. "The 1996 Kaiser Family Foundation Survey on Teens and Sex." 1996.

Horatio Alger Association. "The State of Our Nation's Youth." 1999.

Kilbourne, Jean. *Deadly Persuasion: Why Women and Girls Must Fight the Addictive Power of Advertising.* The Free Press, 1999.

Louis Harris and Associates. "Money Talks!" Girls Inc., 1998.

Louis Harris and Associates. "Re-Casting TV: Girls' Views—A Nationwide Survey of School-Age Children." Girls Inc., 1995.

Hymowitz, Kay. *Ready or Not: Why Treating Children as Small Adults Endangers Their Future—And Ours.* Free Press, 1999.

Newsday. "Early Worries About Weight: Eating Disorders Threaten Kids Unhappy With Their Bodies." March 14, 2000

The New York Times. "Grass-Roots Business." November 28, 1999.

The New York Times. "New Style Maven: 6 Years Old and Picky." September 7, 1999.

The New York Times. "The Face of Teenage Sex Grows Younger." April 3, 2000.

Nichter, Mimi. *Fat Talk: What Girls and Their Parents Say about Dieting.* Harvard University Press, 2000.

Office of Advocacy, U.S. Small Business Administration. "Small Business Profile." 1997.

Pipher, Mary. *Reviving Ophelia: Saving the Selves of Adolescent Girls.* Ballantine Books, 1995.

Presidents's Council on Physical Fitness and Sports. "Physical Activity and Sport in the Lives of Girls." 1997.

Rimm, Jane. *See Jane Win: The Rimm Report on How 100 Girls Became Successful Women.* Three Rivers Press, 2000.

Roper Youth Report. "Kids Make Many Purchase Decisions But Parents' Input Still Counts." 1998.

Shandler, Sara. *Ophelia Speaks: Adolescent Girls Write about Their Search for Self.* HarperPerennial Library, 1999.

Siegler, Ava. *The Essential Guide to the New Adolescence: Raising an Emotionally Healthy Teenager.* Plume, 1998.

Turner, Heather A., and Turner, R. Jay. "Gender, Social Status and Emotional Reliance." *The Journal of Health and Social Behavior.* December 1999.

U.S. Department of Commerce, Bureau of the Census. "Money Income in the United States." 1997.

U.S. Department of Justice. "Prevalence, Incidence, and Consequences of Violence Against Women: Findings from the National Violence Against Women Survey." Washington, D.C., 1998.

U.S. Department of Labor. "Employment and Earnings." 1998.

Wirthlin Worldwide. "Women and Investing: National Quorum." Oppenheimer Funds, 1997.

Women's Bureau. "Women's Earnings as a Percent of Men's (1979–1997)." 1997.

Women's Sports Foundation. "Gender Equity Report Cards." 1997.

Yankelovich Partners Inc. "Generation Cliniques Study: Exploring the New Dynamic Between Mothers and Teen Daughters." Clinique Laboratories, 1998.